Submarines

MODELS AND THEIR ORIGINALS

Submarines

MODELS AND THEIR ORIGINALS

BY CARSTEN HEINTZE

Translated from the original German by Nigel Price

Published by Traplet Publications Limited 2005
Traplet House,
Pendragon Close,
Malvern,
Worcestershire. WR14 1GA
United Kingdom.

ISBN 1 900371 86 3

Printed by Wa Fai Graphic Arts Printing Co., Hong Kong

Contents

About The Author

Carsten Heintze has been a passionate submarine historian, researcher and diver for many years. This book follows on from his other publications. It is set against the background of international research of the third level of the ocean depths and its disciplines of archaeology, biology and history, and flows from his hobby of building fully functional, remote-controlled models of these submarines. The result is a contemporary, technical essay that both traces the history and development of submarines and presents these same submarines as remote-controlled models.

Just like the originals, these models are also unique and occupy a special place in history.

Years of research and support from the author's friends and enthusiastic submarine model-makers have produced an entertaining foray through history, showing the link between yesterday and today and featuring outstanding examples of submarine construction, in the case of both the originals and their models.

The reader learns about the history of the original submarines, finds out where they are today and then is introduced to the models in their element through a wealth of underwater photography.

Almost 80% of the surface of the globe is covered with water, yet we know more about the surface of the moon. So much is still to be discovered...

The author by the "Seahorse".

Chapter 1

The First Manned Diving Vehicle

David Bushnell's 'Turtle'

The original

In 1775, during the American War of Independence, the young Yale graduate, David Bushnell, constructed the 'Turtle' diving-boat. The intention was for the 'Turtle' to be used in the battle against the blockade of the American ports by the Royal Navy.

From the outside the submarine looks like a large, elliptically formed, oak barrel.

The 1:1 reconstruction of the Turtle in the submarine museum in Groton/USA. The external planks are partially removed so that it is possible to see inside the boat. With all the levers required to steer the boat there was little room left inside. In this picture you can clearly see the crank handle for the drill and in the lower section the two brass hand pumps to evacuate the ballast water. You can also see the drum with the rope to let down the lead weight (photo: Marco Kremer).

The approximate dimensions of the boat were: height 2.50 m, length 2.10 m and a beam of 1.20 m.

It was designed to carry only one man and he had to operate all the controls with his hands and feet. The boat was powered by brute strength. A crank handle in front of the operator was connected to a screw on the outside. Steering was via a lever located to his right.

In order to get the boat to dive, water was let into the boat as ballast; two hand pumps were used to expel the water again.

A vertical propeller next to the entry hatch served to support the diving manoeuvre.

A lead weight of approx 75 kg was attached to the bottom of the boat as a base weight. This could be let down on a

A historical drawing of the Turtle. You can clearly see the elements of the propulsion mechanism. However, the artist has been rather generous with the space inside the boat (source NOOA).

Wood and brass – the 'Turtle' is a real picture!

Exploded drawing of the upper section of the 'Turtle'. When submerged this section is above the waterline. It was made from 0.2 mm brass plate. This section of the boat is designed to be free flooding (drawing: Rene Lefevre).

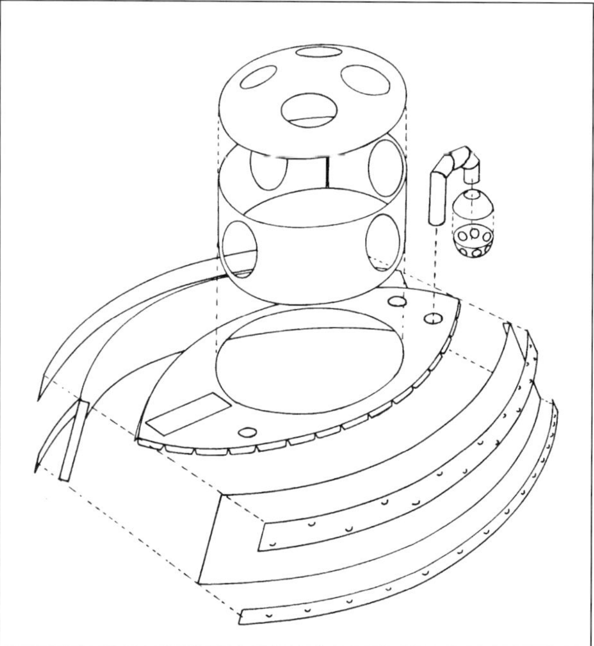

rope approx. 15 metres long to enable the craft to surface in an emergency. Of course, this was only possible if the water depth was less than the length of the rope.

The boat was armed with an externally mounted explosive charge. It was designed so that the operator would use a drill to secure a screw into the rump of an enemy ship. This screw was connected to an explosive charge to be set off using a time fuse.

The 'Turtle's' first deployment came in September 1776 on the East River.

The English navy had laid siege to the port of New York and the task of the 'Turtle' was to approach unnoticed and attach an explosive charge under the navy flagship, HMS Eagle.

Ezra Lee, a young sergeant, was the man brave enough to undertake this venture. The diving boat was towed in the direction of the HMS Eagle. Once it had got as close as possible, the boat was partially flooded and then it continued its journey under manpower, with just the tower sticking out of the water.

According to historical accounts, Ezra Lee is said to have reached HMS Eagle, yet he could not attach the screw for the explosive charge because the ship had a copper plated hull.

He was discovered in his attempt and chased by rowing boats. Struggling desperately against the ebb tide, he did succeed in escaping. As a decoy manoeuvre he had detonated the explosive charge. Apart from a loud bang, this did not cause any damage to the enemy navy.

The 'Turtle' was deployed twice more, each time unsuccessfully, until finally its inventor decided to abandon work on the submarine.

Nothing more is known of where the boat ended up, however two very detailed descriptions enabled a 1:1 scale model to be built and this model can be found today in the submarine museum in Groton/USA.

Our understanding today throws into question whether Ezra Lee ever reached HMS Eagle. For one person to cover the reported distance would require such immense effort that there is every reason to doubt that the attack actually happened in the way it was described. There is also evidence to suggest that HMS Eagle did not get its copper-bottomed hull until some time later.

Nevertheless, today we can still marvel at both the unique design and the individual daring required to venture underwater with this craft.

The 'Turtle' to a scale of 1:10

The model of this early diving boat was built by Rene Lefevre from Belgium, demonstrating his interest in unusual models and his exceptional skill in bringing these to life. His models of the 'Naiade-Class' and the 'Nautilus' are likewise featured in this book.

To a scale of 1:10 the 'Turtle' is only 25 cm high, 21 cm long and has a beam of 12 cm. It has a total weight of 2.5 kg, making it one of the lightweights among model submarines.

The hull of the 'Turtle' is built in two sections. The lower and watertight section consists of a planked timber frame made from 3 and 5 mm plywood. This is made watertight by coating the inside with GRP matting. The outside of the hull is covered with a veneer, coated with several layers of lacquer to make it waterproof. Finally, the top is sealed with a 1.5 mm thick aluminium plate, screwed down tightly with eight screws onto a rubber seal.

Like the original, the 'Turtle' is driven by the two propellers. The motors are fitted with step-down gears to enable

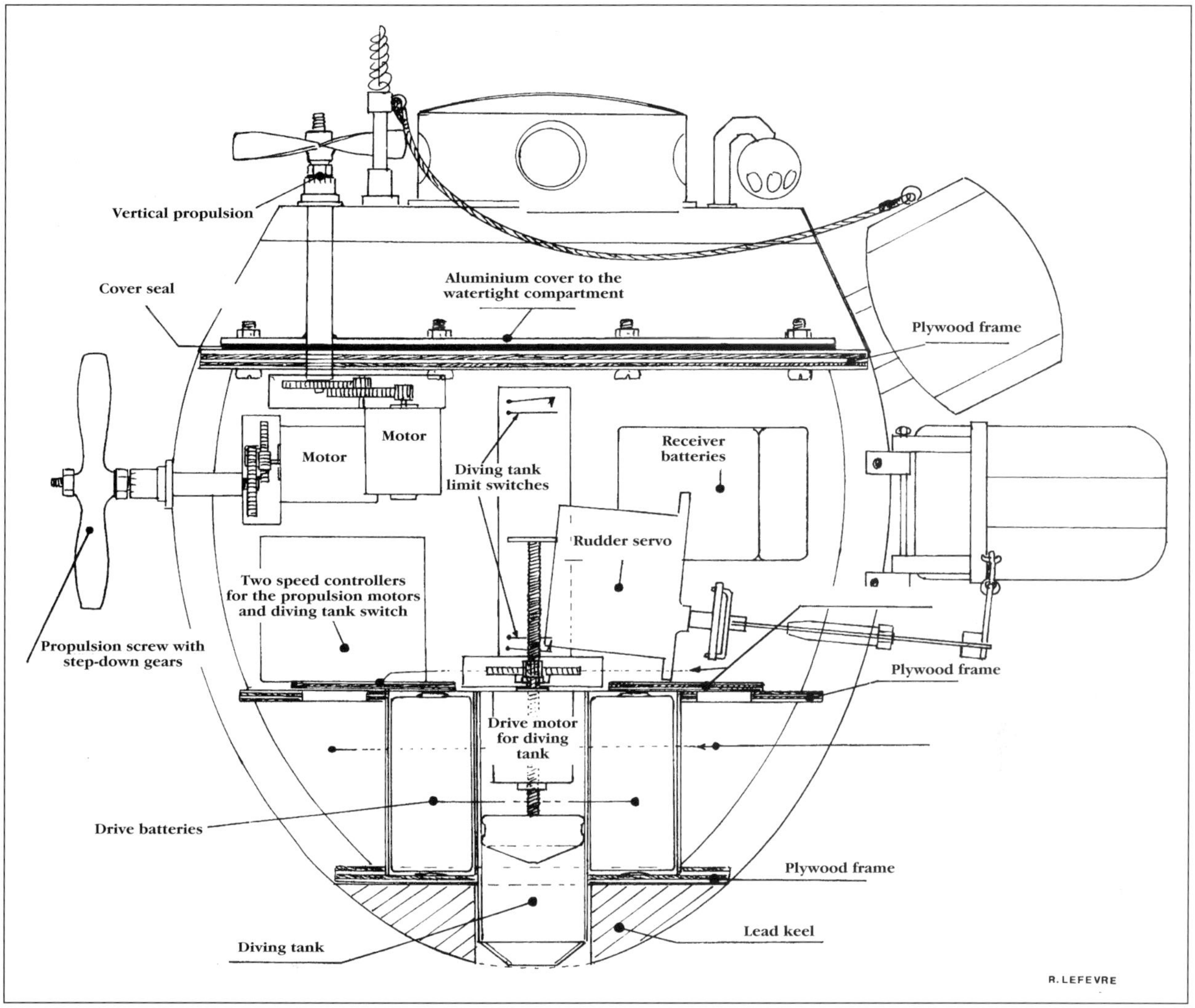

Vertical propulsion
Cover seal
Aluminium cover to the watertight compartment
Plywood frame
Motor
Motor
Diving tank limit switches
Receiver batteries
Rudder servo
Two speed controllers for the propulsion motors and diving tank switch
Propulsion screw with step-down gears
Plywood frame
Drive motor for diving tank
Drive batteries
Plywood frame
Lead keel
Diving tank
R. LEFEVRE

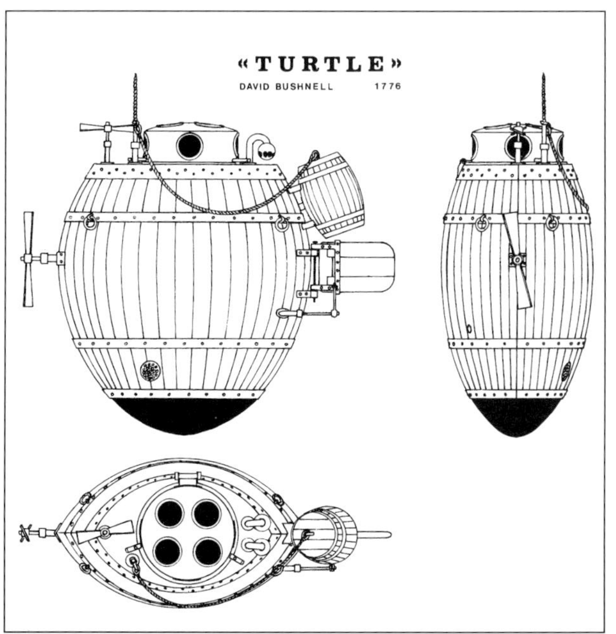

Rene Lefevre's plan drawing of the model in a three-sided view.

«TURTLE»
DAVID BUSHNELL 1776

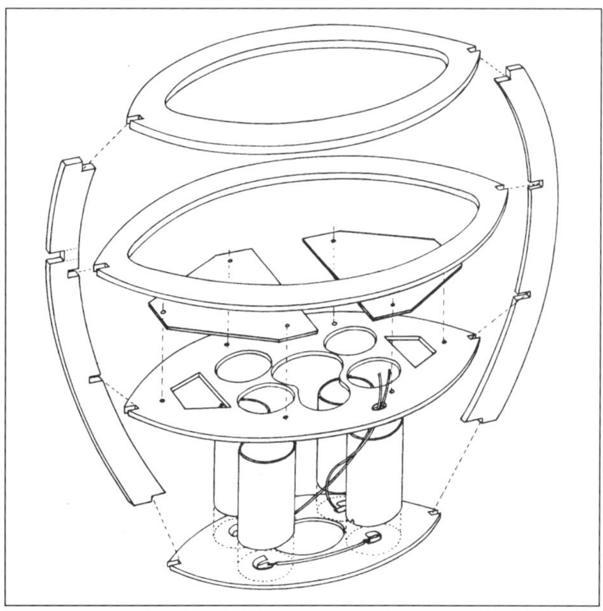

Frame construction of the lower section of the 'Turtle'. You can clearly see the four tubes to take the four NiCd-1.2V/2.2Ah – drive batteries.

The submarine's three main component groups (photo: Rene Lefevre).

When submerged only a small section of the boat can be seen (photo: Rene Lefevre).

View of the lower bottom section with cover and upper deck removed (photo: Rene Lefevre).

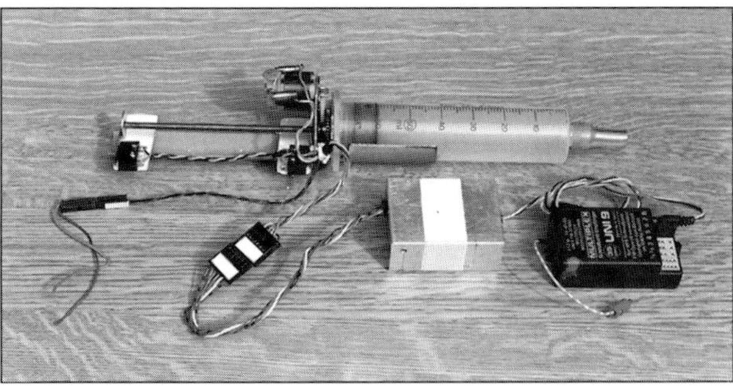

The model's diving tank consists of a 60 cm³ syringe reduced to 40 cm³ with a diameter of 30 mm. It is pulled out or pushed in by an electric motor via a threaded spindle. Two limit switches on the spindle switch off the motors when it is fully flooded or emptied (photo: Rene Lefevre).

the propellers to turn at a speed that is appropriate to the chosen scale.

Robert Fulton's Nautilus

The original

In 1798 the American, Robert Fulton (1765-1815), went to the Directorate in Paris to present his design of the 'Nautilus' diving boat. In his 'History of Submarines' H.J. Lawrence does in fact question whether the design of this boat was all his own work. In 1797 and 1798 Robert Fulton worked as a patent buyer. This often brought him into contact with David Bushnell, who had experience of diving boat design and was living in Paris at the same time.

It was not until 1801 that Robert Fulton was able to build

Three-sided view of the 'Nautilus' – interpretations by Rene Lefevre.

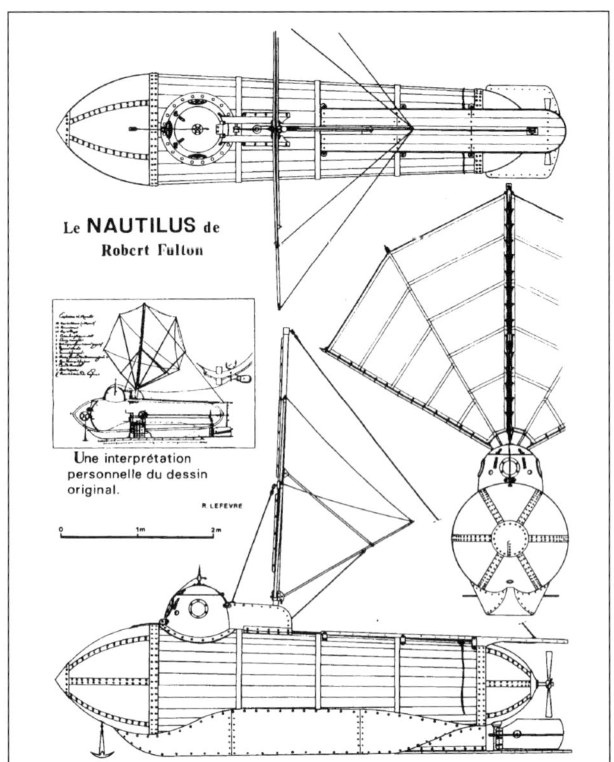

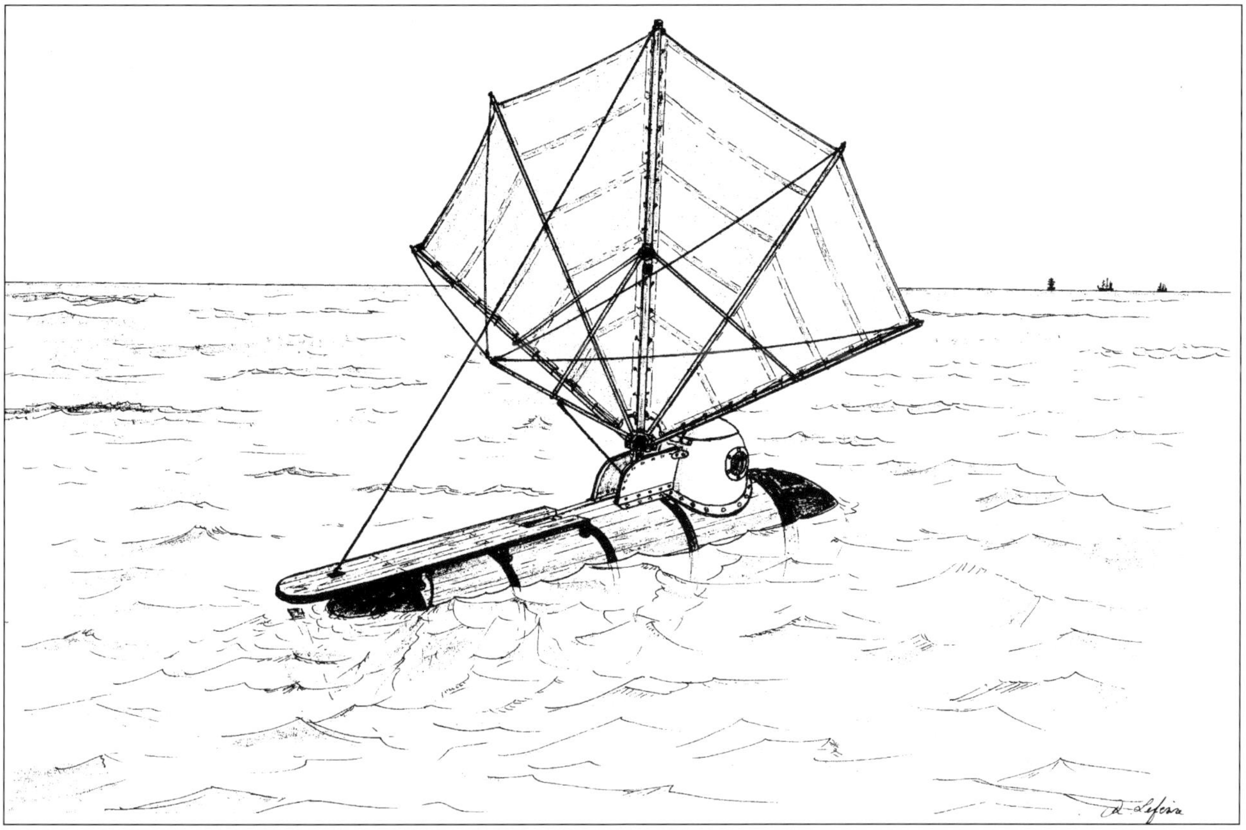

Rene Lefevre has sketched out the 'Nautilus' intended method of deployment. It shows the boat under sail on its way to attack the target ship.

Just out of sight of the enemy ship, the 'Nautilus' submerges.

As soon as it moves into position underneath the hull, a drill is used to secure a screw in the wood. A rope is attached to the eye of the screw and this drags along an explosive charge.

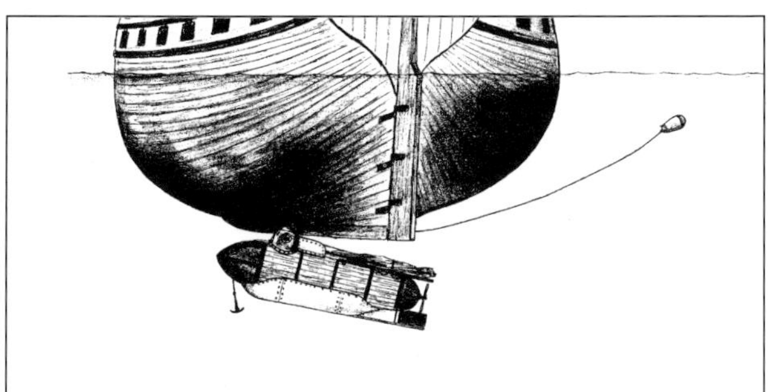

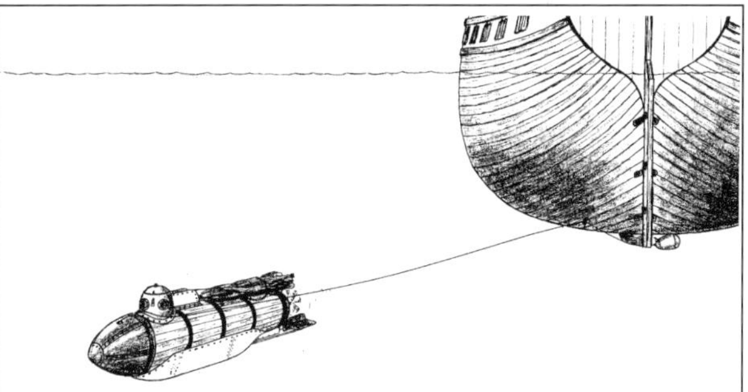

The boat now escapes underwater and in so doing pulls the explosive charge under the ship. Once the boat is at a safe distance away, the explosive charge is set off.

the 'Nautilus' with 10,000 Francs approved by General Bonaparte. The boat was around 6.5 metres long and about 2 m high without the sail. The hull was made of wood with a metal diving tank attached to the bottom. In order to dive, the boat was propelled by turning a crank handle which drove a four-blade propeller.

It can be presumed that two or three crew were required to propel the boat. When sailing surfaced, the 'Nautilus' had a collapsible sail. A rudder was used to steer the boat. It also had a dive plane attached.

It is said that the boat was first tested successfully on June 3rd 1801 in the Seine to a depth of up to 25 feet. It is believed that in the same month the boat was taken to Brest and on June 26th it submerged for one hour to a depth of 8 metres with a crew of four.

Detailed photograph showing the conning tower with the drill (photo: Norbert Brüggen).

Fulton believed that his invention would change the nature of war at sea. The boat was to approach enemy ships underwater and drill a hole in the wooden hull of the ship with a drill. A screw with an eye was fixed into the hull and an explosive charge pulled into position. (The original idea for this attack strategy came from David Bushnell and his 'Turtle'.)

Bonaparte was not convinced by this development and accused him of being a liar and a charlatan. Fulton went to England, France's enemy in war. It is very probable that he destroyed the 'Nautilus' himself before he left on this trip.

In 1805 he had the possibility in England, with the support of a backer in the Admiralty, to present a part of his Nautilus concept, the explosive charge or 'electric torpedo' as he called it. The presentation took place in the Downs, off Walmer Castle in Kent, which was at the time the residence of the Prime Minister, William Pitt. On October 5th 1805 Fulton used a normal boat to pull an explosive charge towards the de-commissioned Danish brig 'Dorothea'. A moment later he confounded the sceptics when the force of the explosion ripped the brig in two and it sank.

Six days later Admiral Nelson won the battle of Trafalgar against the French navy and Great Britain regained its unrestricted naval superiority. With the war at an end Fulton's idea was no longer required. So he went back to America.

During the Anglo-American War of 1812-1814 he tried to sell his submarine plans to the American government. It is understood that underwater attacks were carried out on ships at that time, yet no mention was made whether or not they were successful.

Robert Fulton died on February 24th 1815 and did not witness the launch of his last development, the 'Mute', an 80 feet long submarine with a crew of 100.

Side view of the finished model. All in perfect detail even down to the corresponding stands.

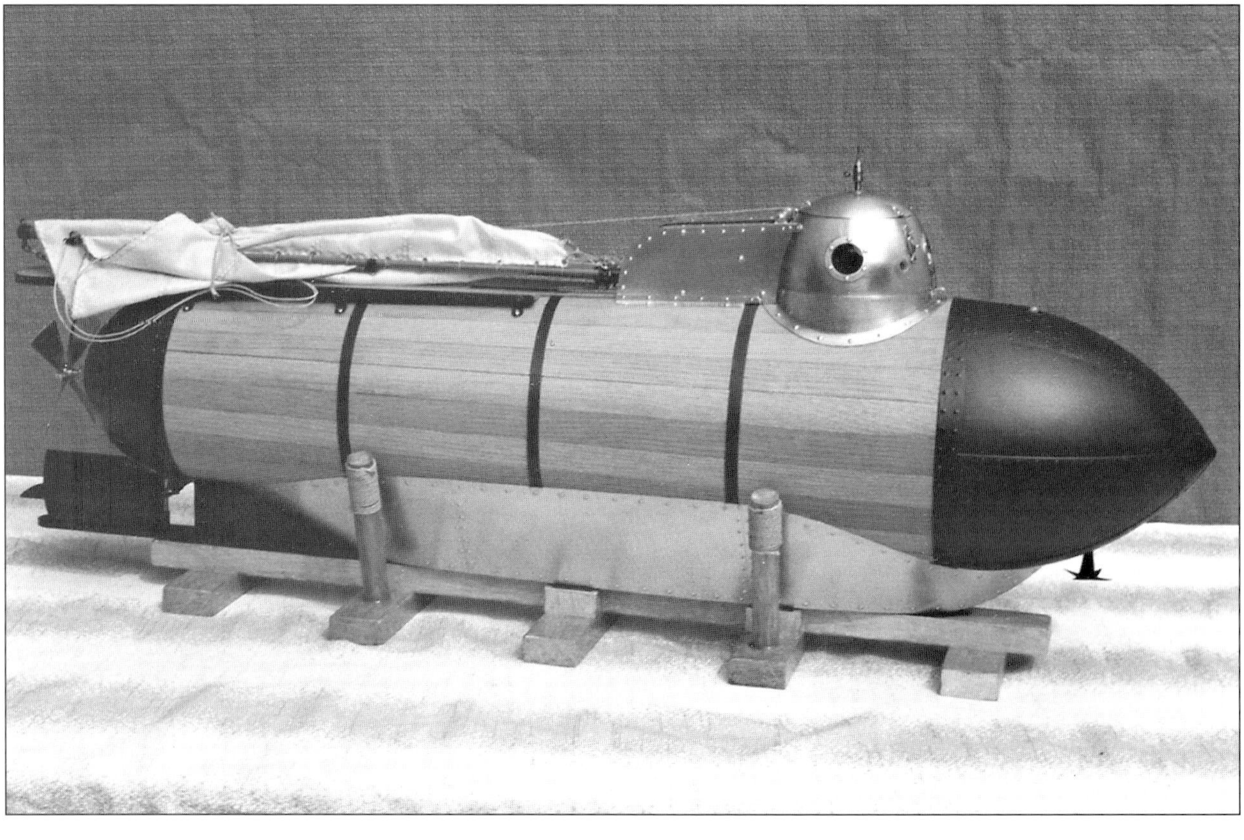

Course set with wind from the stern (photo: Norbert Brüggen).

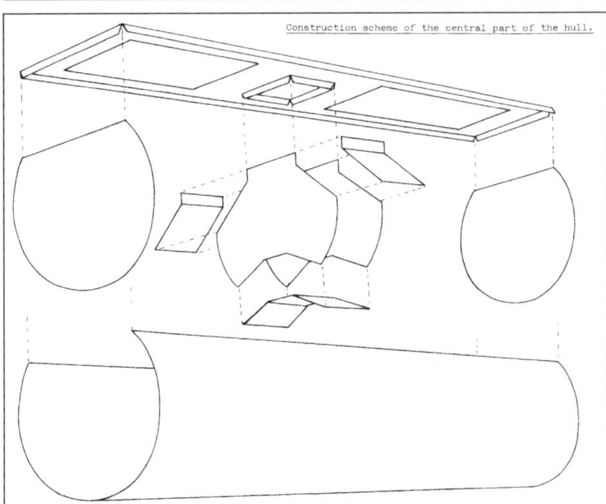

Schematic construction of the central section of the hull. It is built from 0.6 mm sheet steel (drawing: Rene Lefevre).

(photo: Norbert Brüggen).

The shell of the lower section of the hull (photo: Rene Lefevre).

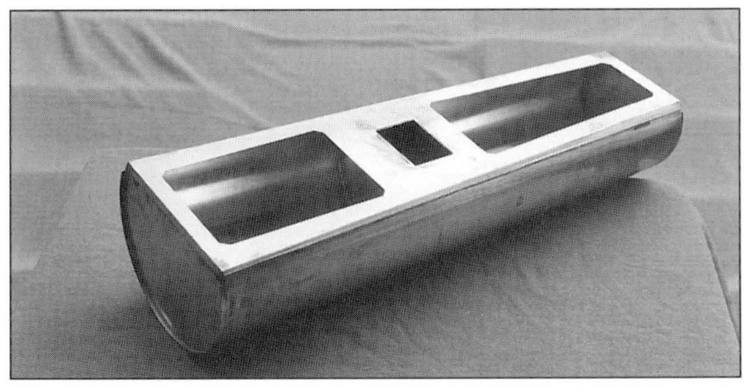

Robert Fulton's Nautilus to a scale of 1:7.5: A model interpretation by Rene Lefevre

Like Rene Lefevre's other two submarines featured in this book, the 'Nautilus' is fascinating to look at. No one had ever before created a submarine with a sail from an almost forgotten time when submarine construction was in its infancy.

The 'Nautilus' is built to perfection. Not only does it look good, it also provides the proof that this design can indeed sail. Expert literature had questioned whether the original was able to do so.

Technical data:

Scale	1:7.5
Length	87 cm
Height of the hull with sail collapsed	75 cm
Weight	12.9 kg
Diving system	A central diving tank with inlet/outlet valve, pressure is provided from a reservoir of butane gas.
Propulsion	A screw with rudder and dive plane beneath.

Right: Stern view of the 'Nautilus' with the four-blade propeller. The dive plane is attached to the rudder (photo: Norbert Brüggen).

Left: The end pieces of the hull were each made of six separate pieces of sheet metal, formed over a wooden mould (photo: Rene Lefevre).

Bottom: The finished sections of the hull (photo: Rene Lefevre).

The mast is folded down, the 'Nautilus' submerges (photo: Norbert Brüggen).

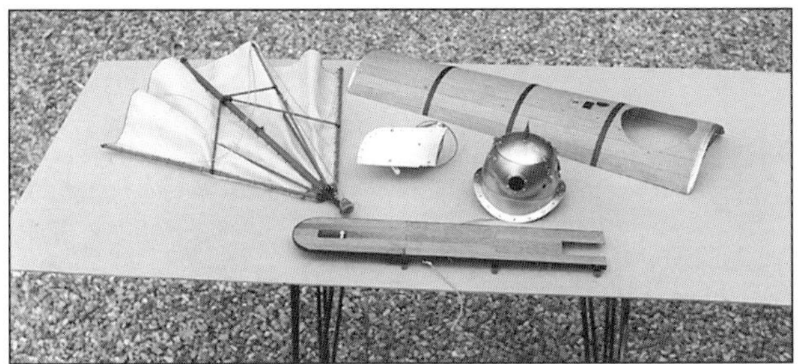

The components that go to make up the upper deck. You can clearly see the sail with its umbrella-like mast mechanism. The sail itself is carefully sewn together from 20 separate pieces of nylon material. Both the upper deck and the hull are covered with an oak veneer (photo Rene Lefevre).

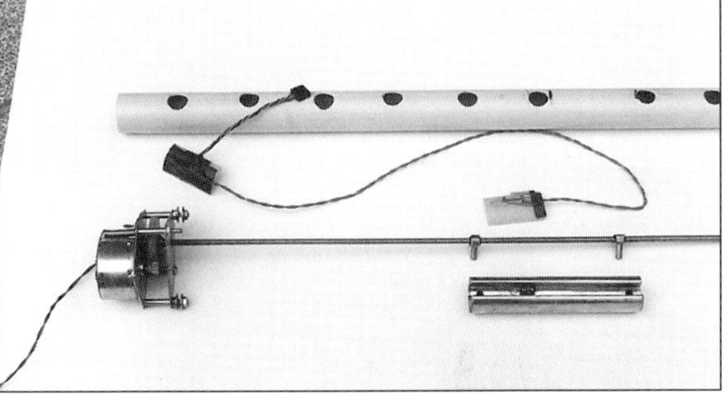

In order to be able to achieve a better horizontal trim, Rene Lefevre incorporated a moveable 200 g trim weight. The lead weight runs on a spindle that is turned by a drive motor (photo: Rene Lefevre).

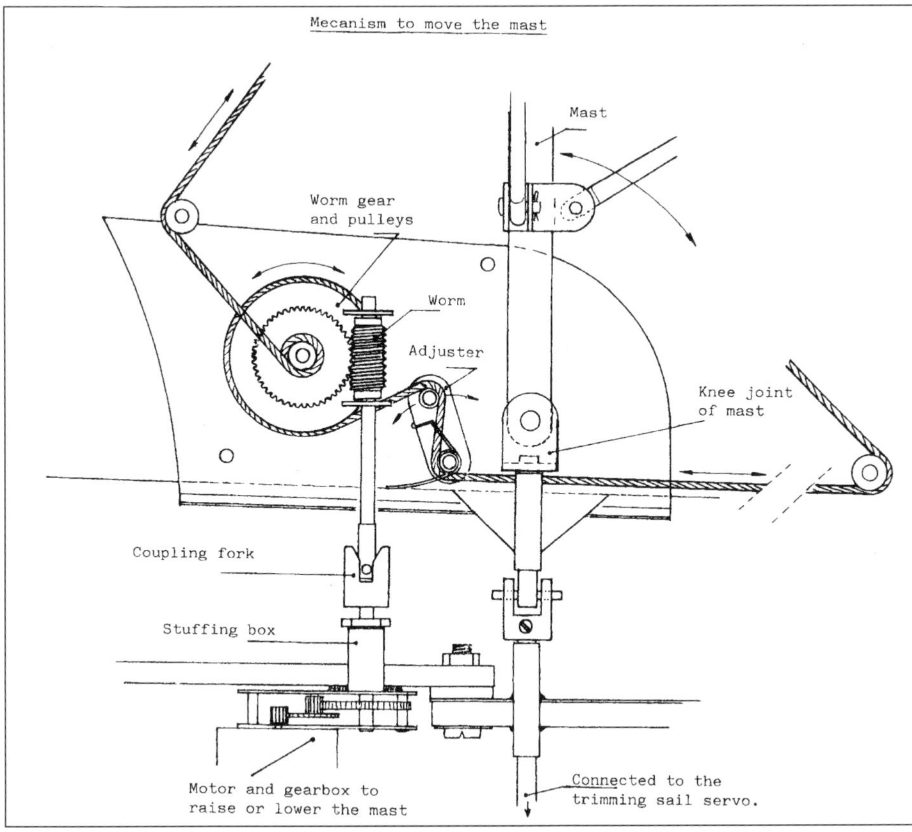

Mecanism to move the mast

Mast

Worm gear
and pulleys

Worm

Adjuster

Knee joint
of mast

Coupling fork

Stuffing box

Motor and gearbox to
raise or lower the mast

Connected to the
trimming sail servo.

Schematic design of the mast mechanism. The mast can be raised using a worm gear; a servo is used to adjust the sail to the wind (drawing: Rene Lefevre).

Wilhelm Bauer's 'Brandtaucher'

The original

In 1850 Wilhelm Bauer, a Bavarian artillery sergeant, developed the first German submersible vehicle, the 'Brandtaucher'.

The idea behind the 'Brandtaucher' came to him on April 13th, 1849 in the course of the battle at the Duppeler Schanzen between the troupes of the German Federation and the Danish army. The concept was for his construction to be able to get close to the pontoon bridge over the Alensund near Soderborg and destroy it. This would eliminate an important supply route for the Danes.

The idea also explains the rather unusual name of the 'Brandtaucher', which was derived from its official name of Brand-Tauch-Apparat (Fire-Dive-Apparatus).

The Brandtaucher was powered by muscle power. Inside there was a gear system with two large hand wheels. They were turned by two of the three crew and drove a screw fixed to the stern of the boat. It was possible to change gear and sail backwards.

At the bow there was a small tower with an entry hatch and four portholes for observation, as well as a hinged opening, fitted with watertight gloves. The opening provides access to position an externally mounted explosive charge.

The boat was built from 6 mm thick, riveted iron plates. The vehicle submerged and surfaced by means of two pumps which forced water into the bilge and then emptied it again. A moveable trim weight of 500 kg was carried on board for the purpose of precise trimming. It was Wilhelm Bauer's intention to use this weight as the load required to dive dynamically into the deep. At that time dive planes, as we

The 'Brandtaucher' arriving at the Kiel Museum of Maritime Transport (photo: Museum of Maritime Transport, Kiel).

know them, were yet to be invented. It was not until some time later that Wilhelm Bauer designed them. So that the submarine was able to submerge, it needed to carry a pig-iron weight on board of approx. 20 t as main ballast. This made it stable for sailing on the surface and gave it a metacentric height of 65 cm.

The first diving trial took place on February 1st 1851 in the port of Kiel. Wilhelm Bauer opened the flood valve and the Brandtaucher began to sink. Due to the absence of separate tanks, the water flowed freely into the bilge and, as dictated by the laws of physics, it accumulated at the submarine's deepest point. Unfortunately this was at the sub's

A contemporary depiction of the 'Brandtaucher in 1851 in front of the construction yard of Schweffel & Howald in Kiel.

(Photo: Franz Baumgartner).

The submarine's stern. The propeller is rebuilt to scale and it is not hard to imagine that turning it must have been particularly hard work.

The submarine's bow and tower section. Here you can see the portholes; the flaps for the watertight gloves were not included. In the original vehicle these were located in front of the side portholes. The bar attached to the bow is a bracket to carry the externally mounted explosive charges. The bracket is found on both the port and starboard side (photo: Franz Baumgartner).

A view of the inside of the model. The boat's control functions are: forwards and backwards, steer left and right. Flood and evacuate the piston-tank. Two 6 volt/10 Ah lead/gel batteries are used to power the boat. These supply a Monoperm motor located underneath. The gear system ensures that the propeller turns at only 480 revolutions/min, which is sufficient to achieve a speed appropriate to scale (photo: Franz Baumgartner).

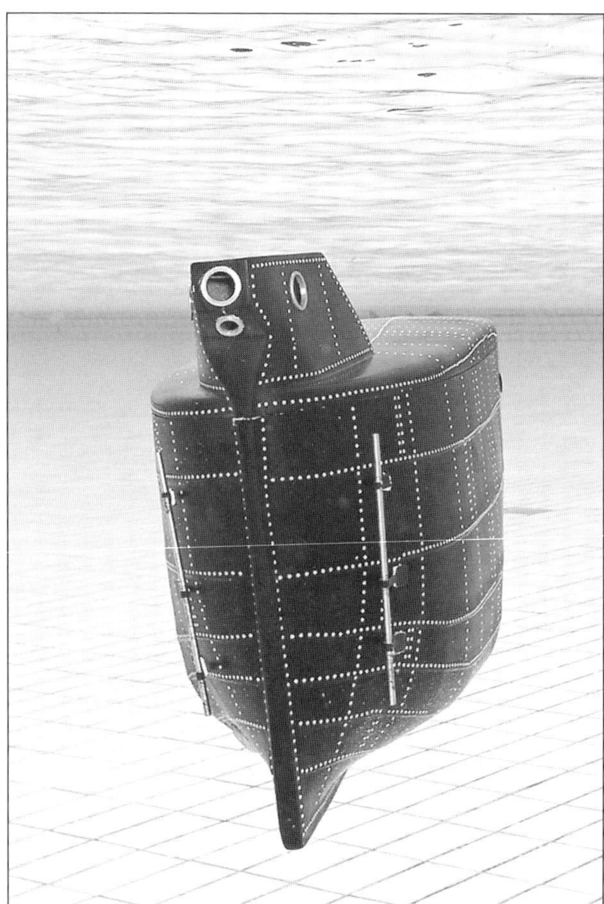

Bow view of the submerged 'Brandtaucher'.

stern. As the load on the stern continued to increase the angle from 28° to 34°, it eventually became too great for the trim weight to correct, and the submarine sank out of control towards the sea bottom.

At a depth of approx. 5.60 metres the pressure was so great that the body of the boat deformed, causing a number of rivets to come out and more water to stream into the hull.

There are no reliable details of just how deep the submarine sank. Wilhelm Bauer used a steam tank boiler as a depth-measuring device. When applied in this way it tends to be a rather imprecise manometer. It can be assumed that the sub came to rest on the sea bottom at a depth between 8.60 and 15 metres. The three men on board were trapped because until the incoming water equalised the external pressure, the 45 cm diameter hatch could not be opened.

Instead of immediately opening the flood valve in order to accelerate the rise to the surface, Bauer waited with his crew of two for at least another six hours until the internal pressure was equal to the external pressure. Not knowing how deep they were, with rising water and the air quality inside worsening considerably, it required tremendous discipline on the part of the three people trapped to wait until Bauer believed that ships would have arrived on the surface to pick them up.

The wait continued for what must have seemed an eternity. Indeed it was a drama that featured in literature of the time. Finally, the three dared to rise to the surface. It became the first time in history that anyone had escaped from a sunken submarine. Wilhelm Bauer and his crew managed to rescue themselves from the deep, while the Brandtaucher was left on the bottom of the sea. Bauer turned his attention to other constructions. Amongst other things he invented what we know today as the dive plane.

However the story of this submarine does not end there. 37 years later in 1887 during dredging work to clear the port for torpedo ships, the Brandtaucher was found in Ellerbeck. The boat was raised and, after touring several exhibitions, found a home in the Museum for Marine Science in Berlin. After World War II it appears to have fallen into disrepair before being restored and ending up in the Army Museum of the GDR in Potsdam. From there its journey took it in 1972 to the Museum of Military History in Dresden. An initiative of the then chairman of the Axel Springer AG, Peter Tamm, brought the boat to Hamburg in 1990, where it was put on display at a specialist exhibition. It was not until the year 2000 that the Brandtaucher returned home to Kiel. For a period of two years it was possible to visit the 'Brandtaucher' in a pavilion of the Kiel Museum of Maritime Transport.

Technical data

Length:	8.07 m
Width:	2.01 m
Average height:	2.86 m
Draught:	2.60 m
Complement:	3

The model

Franz Baumgartner from Vienna took one year to construct his 'Brandtaucher', based on a mould supplied by Rudi Schwarzmeier from Nuremberg. The hull is made from GRP with an internal aluminium frame. The model is built to a scale of 1:10.

It is 80 cm long, 21 cm wide and 32 cm high at the tower. Since it weighs 28 kg, it is obviously not one of those models that you can carry down to the lake under your arm.

However, the scale enables the inclusion of fine detail, such as the effective reproduction of the rivets that were a feature of the original.

For its diving system Franz Baumgartner chose a piston-tank with a volume of 1.1 litres.

The sub is prevented from descending too far by a safety switch connected to a pressure sensor. When it reaches the set maximum depth, the tank is switched to deballast.

Chapter 2

Early Submarine Developments

J.P Holland's No. 9

(Known in the UK as Holland 1)

The original

At the end of the 18th Century the Irish immigrant, J.P. Holland, was one of the most creative forces in submarine development. His work began with the development in 1875 of a pedal powered variant of a diving boat. He had his own company, the Electric Boat Company, based in Groton USA and at the beginning of the 19th century he applied advanced technology to construct the Holland No. 9. For the purposes of simplicity he had numbered his draft designs sequentially in the order in which they were created.

Type No. 9 represented a technical breakthrough. The submarine was 20 metres long and when submerged displaced 120 tonnes. A 160 hp petrol engine provided the forward power when surfaced, while a 70 hp electric motor propelled the submarine when underwater.

A view of the side of the boat, looking from the front. You can clearly see the torpedo tube flap, as well as the poor condition of the metal plating (photo: Carsten Haake).

The Holland No. 9 on display at the Gosport Submarine Museum in 1997. The foundations are already in place for the basin where the submarine will be conserved. At this time the submarine was still freely accessible and to enable easy entry, two door-size openings had been cut into the hull (photo: Carsten Haake).

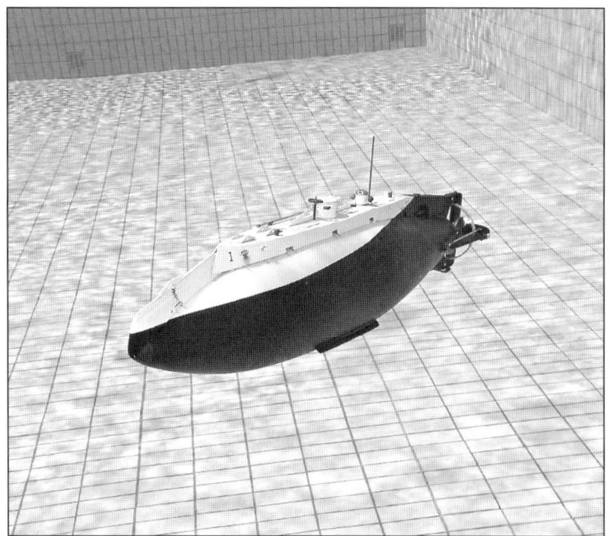

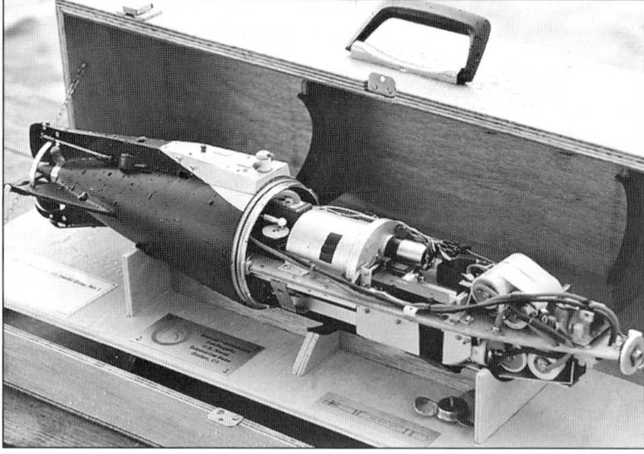

The submarine in its transport box with the front section removed. The equipment frame is easily accessible and at its centre you can clearly see the scratch-built piston-tank, which has a volume of 100 ml. Just in front of this tank to the side is the potentiometer. This controls the position of the piston spindle and enables a proportional flooding and deballasting of the tank. A Brüggen pitch controller is also integral to the diving system. The submarine is propelled by a 72 watt Bühler motor, which directly drives the shaft via a power grip clutch. The submarine's screw is scratch-built.

The electric motor was supplied by 60 cells, developing a total of 120 volts and 1,840 Ah.

Both motors drove a shaft/screw via a gear system. A combination-type propulsion system, as is usual today with diesel-electric motors, was likewise possible. The maximum range surfaced was 560 nm. at a speed of 6 knots. When submerged, it reduced to 35 nm. at a speed of 5.5 knots. The maximum speed surfaced was 8.5 knots and submerged 7 knots. Midships the sub had three diving tanks and there was a trim tank in both the bow and the stern.

The design of the submarine was such that even with its tanks flooded it still retained a degree of buoyancy. This was counteracted by means of dynamic diving. It was armed with Whitehead torpedoes, which could be fired through the bow torpedo tube.

Side view of Holland No.9. The light marking clearly indicates the waterline and shows that the submarine is trimmed to be weighted on the aft. The two front masts served as ventilation masts on the original. Partially hidden behind the second mast, you can see the wheel used to steer the submarine when surfaced. The mast behind it is the periscope. Further to the aft you can see the compass and right next to it the battery ventilation mast. On the right of the picture is a scale figure to illustrate the submarine's comparative size (photo: Carsten Haake).

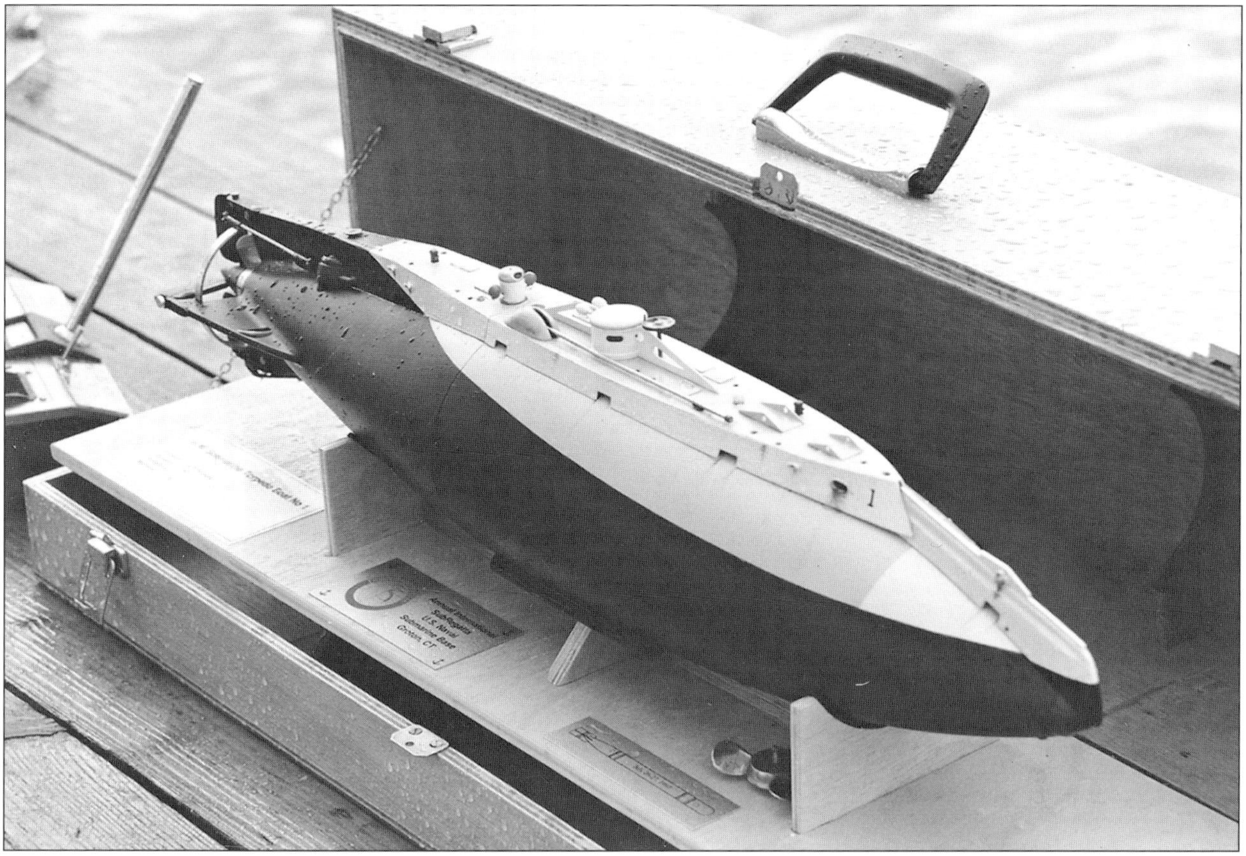

The front section of the hull has been replaced and the boat is ready to go. On the deck you can see the collapsible periscope and a number of rust marks that give the paint coating a realistic feel.

In order to compensate for the weight difference that this causes, the boat has additional trim tanks.

Whilst the British Navy declared this submarine to be an unfair weapon, it did not stop the Royal Navy from building five boats of this type from 1901 onwards. Not one of these boats was lost in service. The first boat was in service for twelve years, until in 1913 the decision was taken to scrap it. On the way to the scrapyard the hawser broke near Plymouth and the submarine foundered and sank to the depths of the English Channel.

Detailed view of the stern. The complicated rudder steering operates by means of a lever. The rudder on the original was steered in the same way (photo: Carsten Haake).

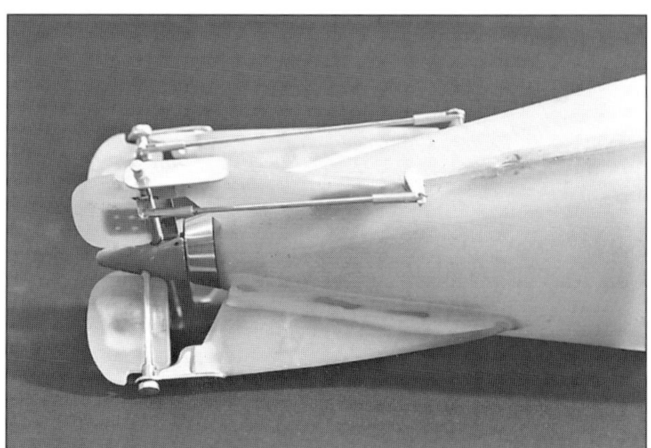

68 years later on April 14th, 1981 the Royal Navy minesweeper HMS Bossington came across the submarine again in the Channel and some time later it was brought back to the surface. The submarine was still in relatively good condition and it was put on display in the Gosport Submarine Museum.

Unfortunately, the people at Gosport had no experience of how to effectively preserve the submarine over an extended period with it left open to the elements. After 15 years this lack of the appropriate knowledge resulted in the condition of the submarine deteriorating to such an extent that there were a number of rust holes in the pressure hull and the steel plate had become paper-thin. In an effort to put

Half power ahead, the sub starts its dive.

a halt to this deterioration, work started in 1995 to construct a basin around the submarine. The basin would contain a liquid and when submerged in this liquid the submarine should be lastingly preserved for the next 10 years.

J.P. Holland's company, the Electric Boat Company, still exists today. It built the 'Nautilus', the world's first nuclear submarine, and today continues to construct the most advanced nuclear-powered submarines.

The Model

Carsten Haake from Bremerhaven built a model of the Holland No. 9 to a scale of 1:30, based on a plan he found in the British specialist magazine 'Model Boats'.

He first made the desired hull shape from wood and then used this as a mould to create the model's hull from GRP.

The individual elements of the deck are made from printed circuit board material, which was then soldered over the skeleton frame. To create the impression of rivets and plates, Carsten Haake used a copper foil, which he worked with a pinwheel and then adhered to the deck.

The model is 60 cm long and displaces 4 kg. The line that divides the removable top from the sub's bottom section is located at the height of the compass base. To seal the submarine he uses a bayonet ring with a diameter of 120 mm.

Sweden's first U-boat The 'Hajen'

The Original

The Swedish engineer Cars Richson designed the 'Hajen' in 1903. It was the Swedish Navy's first submarine. The sub looks very similar to the American Holland designs of the same period, but was not made under licence. Cars Richson had worked for several years in the US as an engineer for J.P. Holland. The experience he gained there certainly influenced the construction of the 'Hajen'. The boat entered service in 1904.

Initially the 'Hajen' was fitted with an advanced petroleum engine developing 200 hp. Later this was removed and replaced by a modern 135 hp diesel engine. In the course of this refurbishment new accumulators were installed and the length of the submarine was increased by 1.8 metres. In 1909 and 1910 three further submarines of the same type were built. The 'Hajen' was withdrawn from service in 1922. Since 1932 it has been on display at the Karlskrona Naval Museum in Sweden and remains the best-preserved submarine of its time.

Technical data:

Length:	23.4 m
Width:	3.6 m
Displacement when submerged:	111 t
Propulsion	135 hp diesel engine/ 70 hp electric motor.
Operational range surfaced	640 nm.
Speed	surfaced 9.5 knots, submerged 6.5 knots
Dive depth	30 m
Complement	12 crew
Armament	one torpedo tube, 3 torpedoes.

The 'Hajen' in the Karlskrona Naval Museum (photo: Stefan Lipsky).

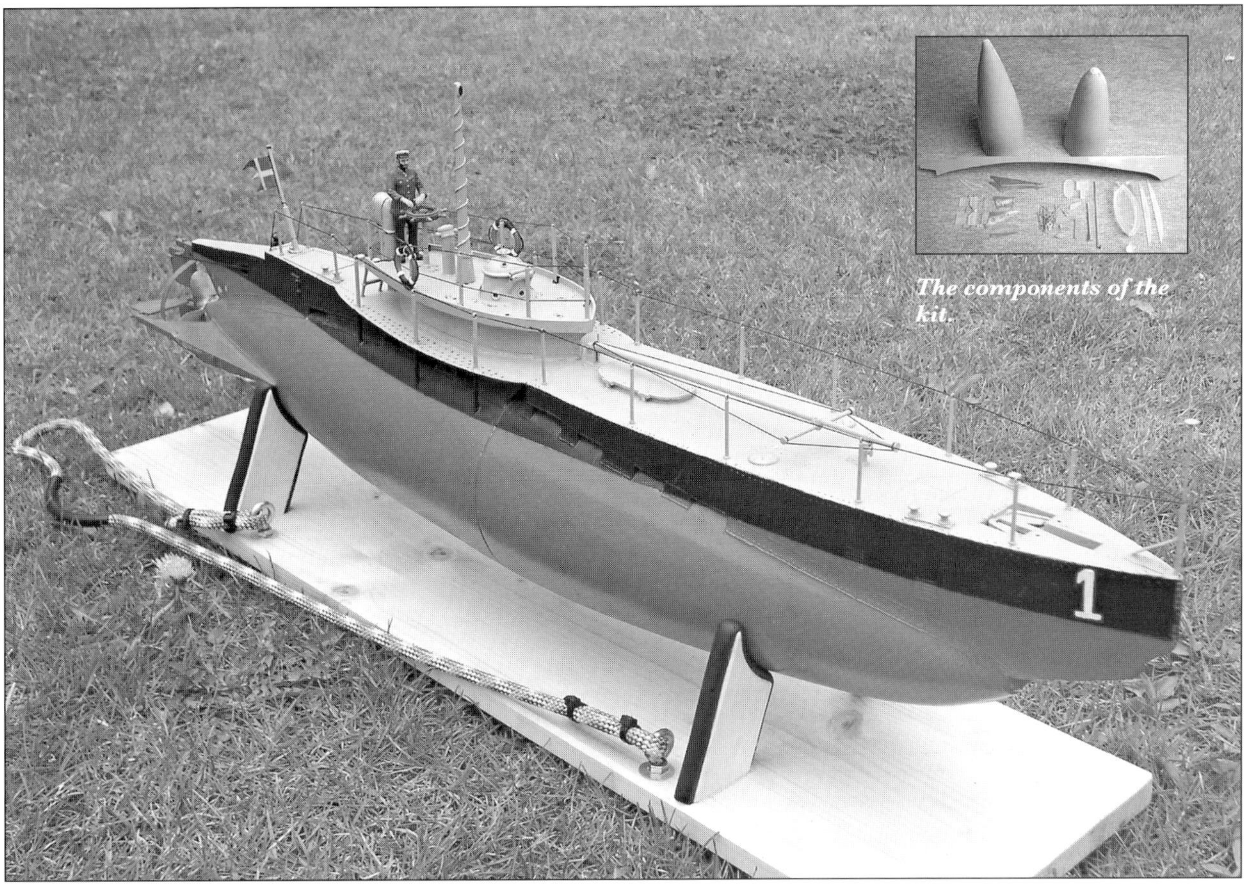

The components of the kit.

The 'Hajen' on its transport stand.

The model

SONAR member Norbert Heinrichs has a soft spot for submarines that are a little bit out of the ordinary. This has produced models of the U-Deutschland and the British C-Class from the beginning of the 20th century. So it came as no surprise that he was interested in obtaining the hull of the 'Hajen' from Norbert Brüggen Modell-U-Boot-Spezialitäten and became the first person to construct a pre-series model of this extraordinary submarine.

The conning tower and upper deck recreated in loving detail.

The model's hull is made in two sections from GRP. The construction kit includes the deck, conning tower, rudder, masts and railings. A scratch-built bayonet lock is used to join the bow and stern together. The submarine's remote control components are mounted on an equipment plate, which is fixed into the front section of the bayonet lock by two M8 threaded bolts.

View of the inside of the submarine. You can clearly see the equipment plate and the two ballast bags.

Full steam ahead and looking good.

The speed controller, the receiver and the dive pump controller, including hose pump and both ballast bags, are all mounted on the equipment plate. Originally it was intended to incorporate a piston-tank. However, this would have required a flood volume of approx. 1 litre and consequently was too big for the submarine. Therefore the alternative diving system of the hose-pump with two 400 ml ballast bags was chosen. The bags are made from pond liner, which is cut to size and stuck together. The only disadvantage of this system is that it takes a little longer to flood and deballast the system and this in turn also makes it impossible to achieve a precise trimming. Located underneath the technical plate is the lead-gel, 12 volt/2 Ah drive battery and the NiCd 6 volt, 2.100 mAh receiver battery. The servos for the rudder and dive planes are screwed into the hull with brackets and drive externally protruding rods via stuffing boxes.

The 'Hajen' is powered by a 720 Hopf motor that is screwed down into a cone-shaped motor frame. A special feature is the design of the fixings: the motor is easy to replace, simply by turning two star-handles. A comprehensive account of how Norbert Heinrich built his 'Hajen' appeared in 'Modell Werft' 6/2003.

(Drawing: Rene Lefevre).

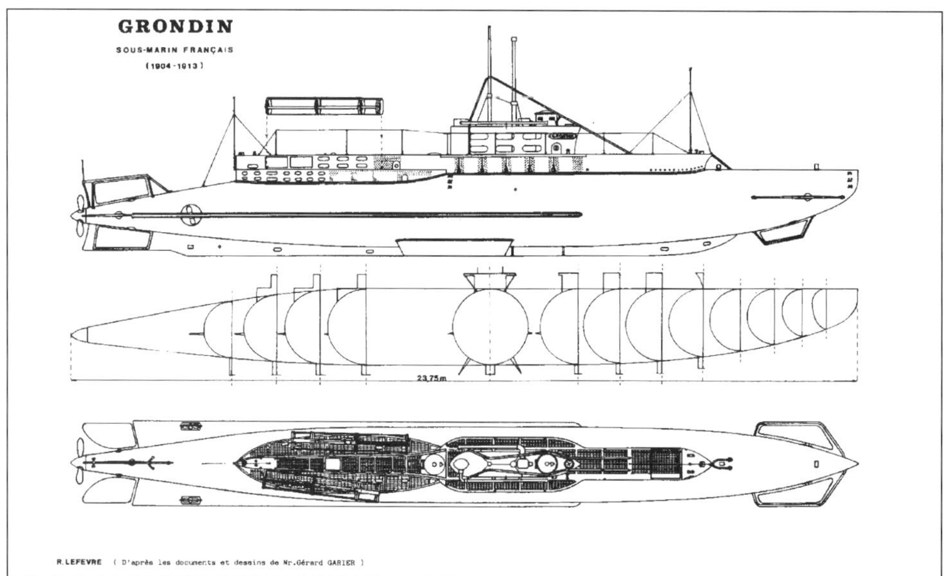

The French Naiade Class Submarines

The Originals

The 20 Naiade class submarines (named after the first boat in the series) were designed in 1900 by the naval architect Romazotti as electric powered single-hull submarines. They formed part of the French Navy's construction programme and entered service in 1904/1905.

They were used for training and for the defence of the ports of Dunkirk, La Rochelle, Toulon, Bizerte and also Saigon.

Although they were small and not very fast – surfaced 7.2 knots and submerged 6 knots – these submarines were of considerable technical interest and had several notable features. Just like their forerunners 'Morse' and 'Farfadet', this class had a variable pitch propeller and two lateral propellers located towards the stern. These forerunners of a bow or stern jet rudder gave the boat an impressive manoeuvrability. Locating the main propeller behind the rudder was also particularly beneficial.

The final element of this design was another rudder under the bow.

A single electric motor provided the main propulsion.

When surfaced, two petrol engine units were switched to supply voltage to the electric engine and to charge the batteries.

This propulsion system enabled it to travel distances of up to 200 nautical miles.

Whilst accidents did occur, no submarine was lost in the 10 years that this type of submarine was in service and there were no fatalities.

Three of the submarines were withdrawn from service in 1912, the remainder in 1914.

The 'Alose' on the COMEX site (photo: COMEX).

Technical data:	
Displacement	surfaced 70 t, submerged 73.6 t
Length	23.75 m
Width	2.26 m
Propulsion	single shaft
Speed	surfaced 7.2 knots, submerged 6 knots
Range	max. 200 nautical miles
Armament	two torpedoes in external tubes
Complement	13 crew
Operational dive depth	30 m

The 'Grondin' (photo: Rene Lefevre).

The upper deck raised and viewed from below (photo: Rene Lefevre).

Function of flood and control valve (drawing: Rene Lefevre).

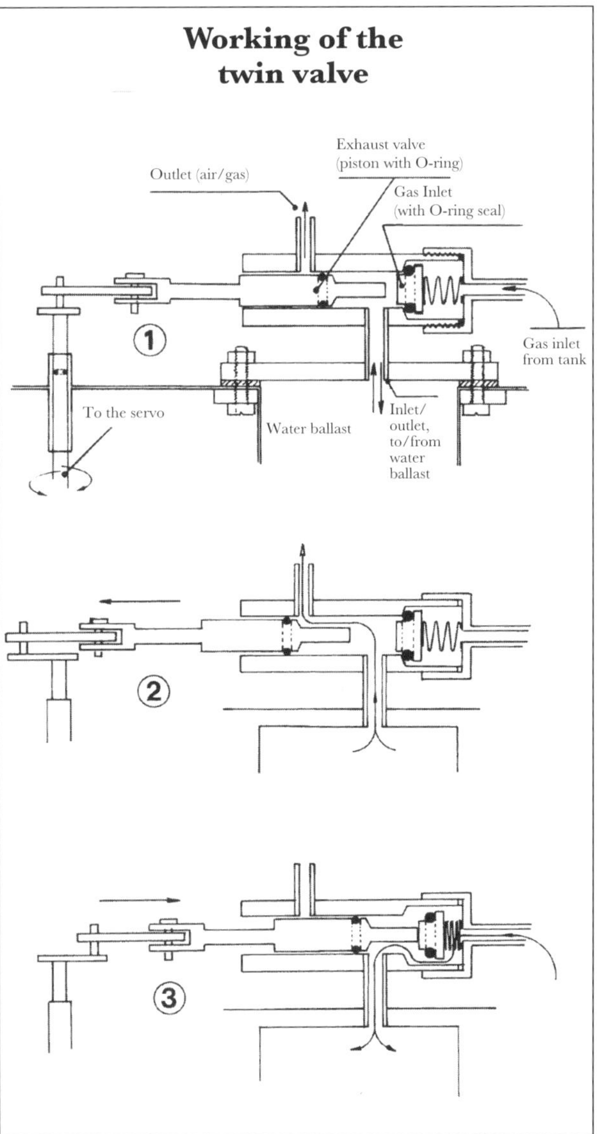

Cross-section of diving tank
(drawing: Rene Lefevre)

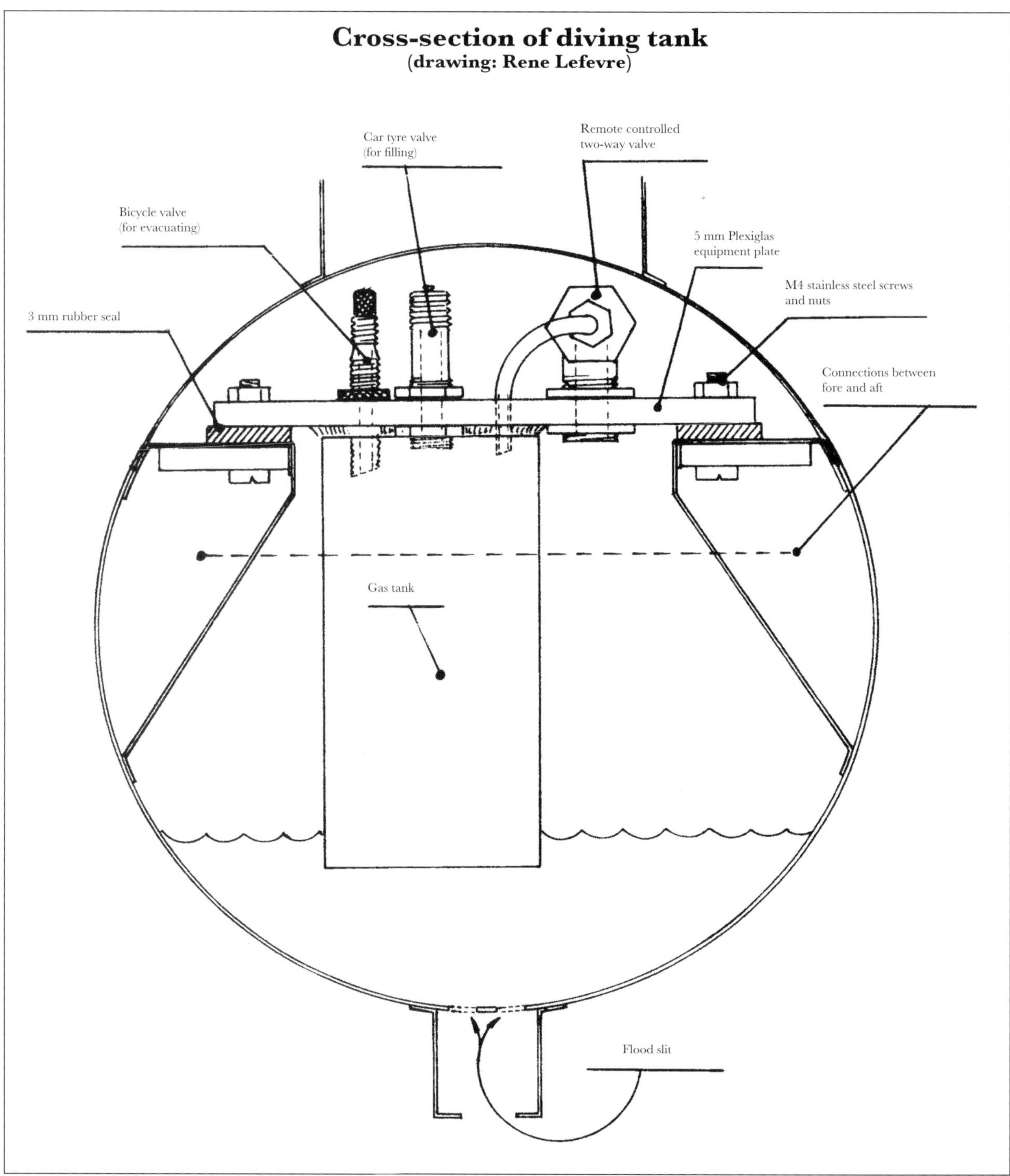

The 'Alose'

The 'Alose' was one of the Naiade class submarines that was withdrawn from service in 1914. It was not scrapped, but was sunk in 1918 by two bombs when acting as a target in an exercise conducted by the French Air Force on the coast of Saint Raphael (Cote d'Azur).

57 years later in 1975 Jean Pierre Joncheray, a member of the 'Societe Archeologique Subaquatique' found a large unknown metallic object on the sea bottom at a depth of 56 metres. It was the 'Alose' and it stood upright on its keel in the mud. 12 months later the 'Alose' was raised by the French company, COMEX. The pressure hull had survived and was restored and today can be seen on the COMEX site in Marseille.

The Model

The 'Alose' is based on her sister ship 'Grondin'. It was built by Rene Lefevre, a Belgian model-submarine enthusiast. He also provided the author with complementary historical information about these submarines.

The model is constructed to a scale of 1:16; it is 1.48 m long and weighs 12.5 kg. The original boats were painted in

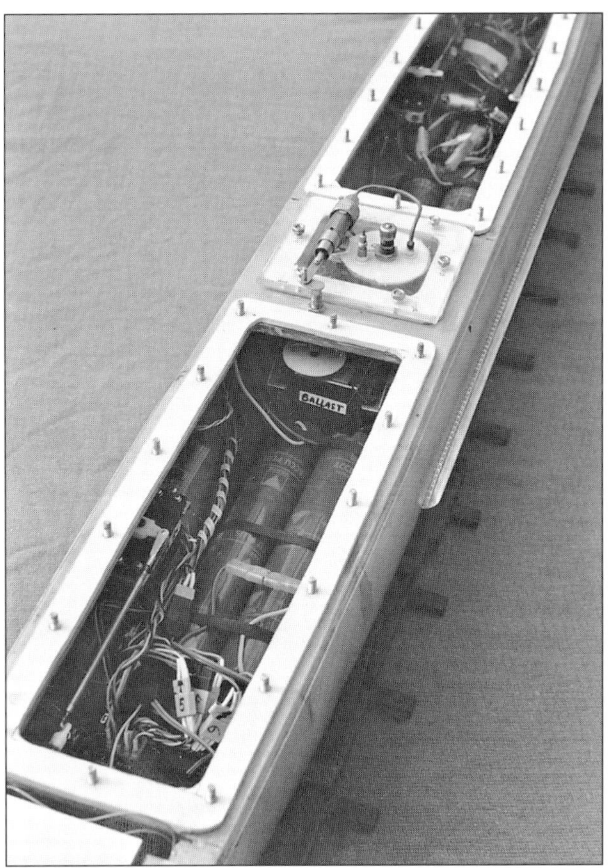

Top: The model's gas tank removed; to the right you can see the opening to the diving tank (photo: Rene Lefevre).

Right: View of the inside of the submarine. The upper deck and the Plexiglas covers have been removed, revealing the pressure resistant compartments containing RC equipment.

Bottom: Section through the hull (drawing: Rene Lefevre).

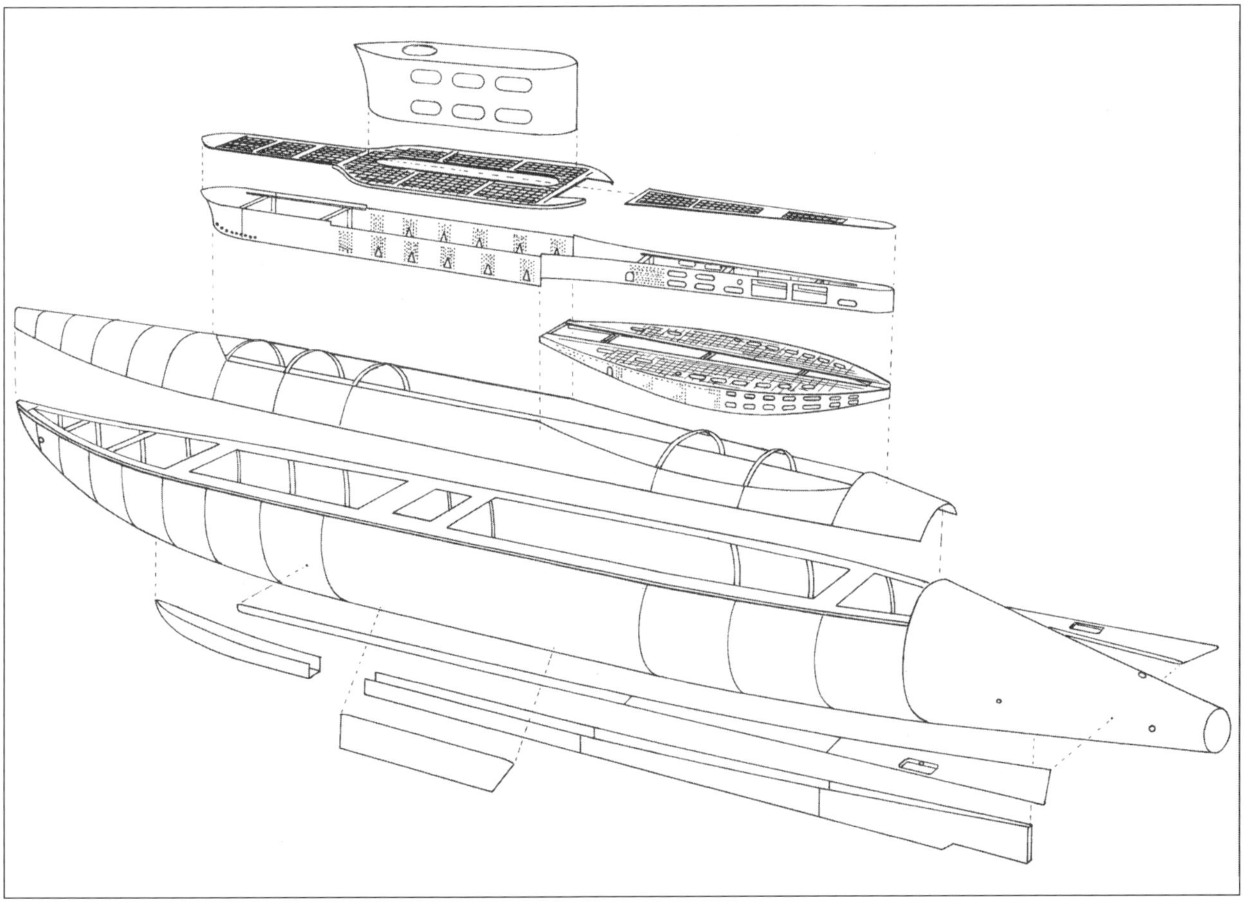

Detailed photograph of the stern. You can clearly see one of the two lateral propulsion systems (photo: Rene Lefevre).

two shades of green; a dark green under the waterline and a bottle green above. However, Rene's modelling friends so liked the optical effect created by the metal construction that they persuaded him not to paint the boat. However, this resulted in greatly increasing the tendency for oxidation and the only solution was to paint it after all. Consequently, it can no longer be seen with its attractive metal finish, as on the photographs here.

The hull is built from 0.6 mm zinc plate and 0.2 and 0.3 mm brass plates, which go to make up the hull plating around 13 main frame supports.

In order to minimise the volume of the diving tank, Rene Lefevre simply chose to create a watertight central section around 80 cm in length, in which he located all the boats electronic and mechanical components.

This central compartment is divided in two by the diving tank which has an approximate volume of 500 ml. Butane gas was chosen as the buoyancy source. The sketches clearly show how this principle works.

The model's technical features:	
Main propulsion motor	JFJ 12 v/30 watt
Batteries	Nicad 12 v/5 Ah
Control functions	Speed controller (ahead and astern), rudder (bow and stern), lateral propeller, front dive planes, gas tank valve, pitch/depth controller, emergency discharge of lead ballast.

View of the conning tower and the external torpedoes (photo: Rene Lefevre).

Chapter 3

World War II Submarine Developments

'U25' – U-boat type Ia

For several years Krick, the model supplier, has included in its range a broad replica of the submarine type Ia from 1937. In contrast to most of today's submarine model kits the lower hull of the Ia consists of a wood sandwich construction. The hull cover and the upper deck are made of ABS. Flood slits have already been milled out of the upper deck. The cost of the model is not excessive and the boat provides a good way of getting into this hobby.

When building the model, it is vital that the wooden hull be properly sealed with lacquer; obviously water quickly has rather an adverse effect on bare wood. A permanent alternative, which will also withstand the odd 'knock' in the pool, involves laminating the hull with a thin GRP mat. This requires a little extra effort, but it proved very well worthwhile for my model.

The 'U25' dives purely dynamically. This means that forward motion and the setting of the front dive plane causes the model to dive, while it begins to rise as soon as forward propulsion stops. This dynamic dive process means that the technical equipment is similarly straightforward. Propulsion comes from two 400-class electric motors driving two propellers. The motors are powered by two 6 volt/3.4 amp lead-gel batteries connected in series, with a BEC speed controller taking the required receiver voltage from the drive battery. A servo is required to control each of the dive planes and rudder. This means that the model can be operated using a competitively priced, 3-channel remote control device. A pitch controller connected to the dive plane improves the model's

The model with well executed camouflage paint.

In 'heavy seas' you do need to look a bit closer.

handling. This controller has the function of maintaining the required dive depth by means of an inclinometer and to compensate for up or down movements in the model when in motion.

Dimensions	
Length	108 cm
Width	75 cm
Height	23.5 cm

The use of Norbert Brüggen's pitch controller proved to be effective in this application.

In terms of its handling characteristics this model is pretty quick off the mark. The maximum speed is much higher than that of the full-scale vessel.

U-Boat Type VIIc

A visit to the 'U 995' museum submarine in Laboe

The Type VII submarines are the most common and

The U 995's conning tower with the two anti-aircraft platforms (wintergarten). At the front of the tower above the wave breaker you can see the bracket for the snorkel mast.

The submarine's four torpedo tubes. A setting computer can be seen at the back in between the tubes; this drives the torpedo mechanically via flexible shafts.

The port rear view of the submarine.

well-known World War II submarines. The Type VII was developed from the Type Ia and was designed as a twin hull submarine.

Of the 709 submarines of this series there is only one left in Germany, the U 995.

After the end of the war this submarine was given to Norway by way of reparation. It was in service there until 1965 as the 'S 309 U-Kaura'.

As a gesture of reconciliation the boat was returned to Germany in 1965. Under the watchful care of the German Navy Federation it was found a home on the beach at Laboe as a memorial and technical museum. A visit to the boat is a must. It gives an impression of that period in history and shows what conditions were like for the submarine crew.

The following photo-tour is intended to provide a brief impression.

Technical data

Total length	62.73 m
Beam	6.203 m
Diameter of the pressure hull	4.70 m
Displacement	surfaced 769 tons submerged 871 tons
Operational dive depth	120 m
Maximum dive depth	200 m
Maximum speed	surfaced 17 knots, submerged 7.6 knots
Range at cruising speed	7,900 nm. at 10 knots
Range with electric motors (submerged)	80 nm. at 4 knots/130 nm. at 2 knots
Diesel oil fuel tank capacity	113.47 t
Complement	45-52 crew.

The stern torpedo tube in the U 995's electric engine room. A reserve torpedo could be stored under the floor plates. The electric compressor can be seen in the right of the picture. This is the location for the entry to the museum submarine.

A view of the two diesel engines.

The port side diesel engine controls. At the top edge of the photograph you can see the engine telegraph, next to it the temperature monitor for each of the cylinders. The diesel engines were started by compressed air.

The switch panel for the starboard electric motor.

Further towards the stern after the galley are the adjoining living and sleeping quarters for the warrant officers. You can see the guardrails attached to the bunks. These were intended to prevent the crew rolling out of their bunks in heavy seas. Small cupboards are fixed to the wall for storage of personal effects and clothing. There was only room for the essentials. This area was closed off from the control room by the pressure resistant bulkhead.

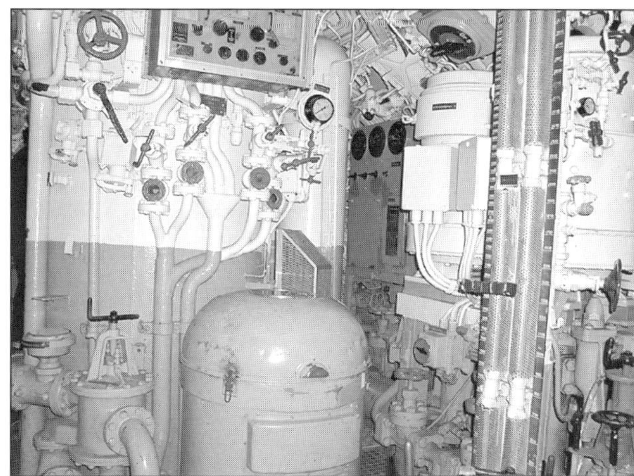

A view of the rear section of the control room showing the main housing for the gyrocompass.

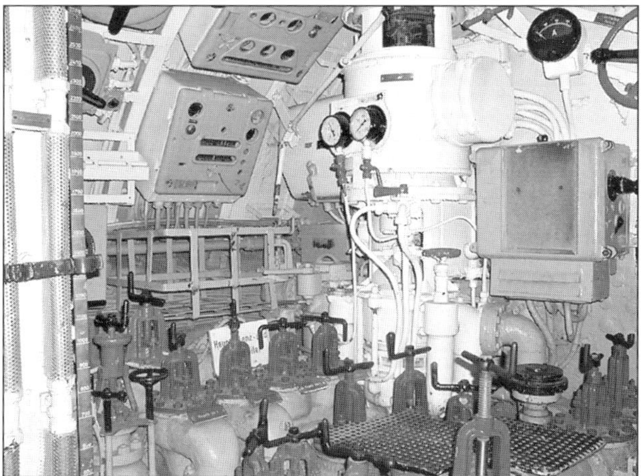

The main deballast and flood manifold on the rear starboard side of the control room.

The submarine's trim station. It is located in the front part of the control room next to the dive plane controls on the starboard side.

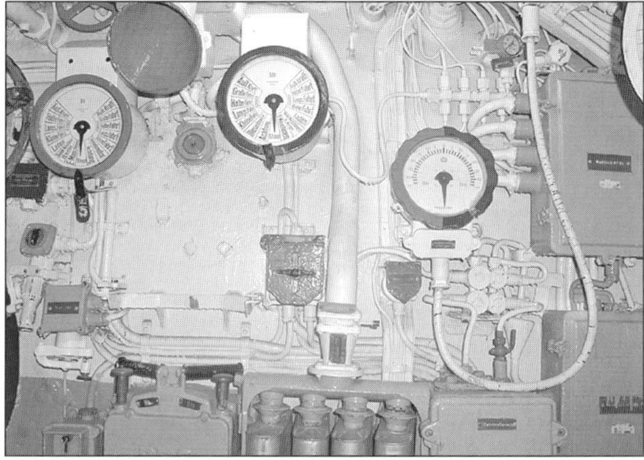

The rudder control area on the end wall of the control room. The rudder is operated by means of push buttons. At the top of the photograph you can see the engine telegraphs for the port and starboard engines. To the right of these is the rudder position indicator. The four metal canisters next to the rudder housing contain breathing lime and are connected to the boat's air purification system.

The controls for bow and stern dive planes in the control room. They are also operated by push buttons, although the hand wheels that encircle them can be used to move the planes if the system fails. Between both planes is the 'Papenberg'. This is a glass tube, filled with liquid, that indicates the height of the conning tower above the water surface and therefore enables an accurate adjustment of the height of the periscope or snorkel. The plane position indicators are located above the plane controls. You can also see the 20 metre precision depth gauge on the left and above it the two engine telegraphs and the depth gauge for larger depths up to 220 m.

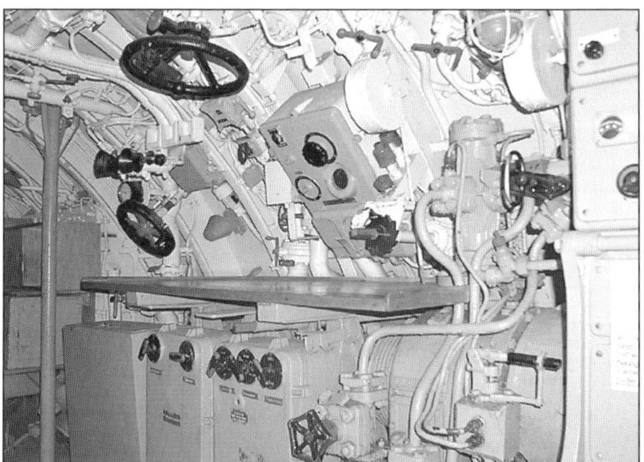

The chief coxswain's navigation table on the port side of the control room. Steering devices for the torpedo armaments are located beneath this table.

A view of the radio room. This is where radio messages were deciphered using the enigma-code machine.

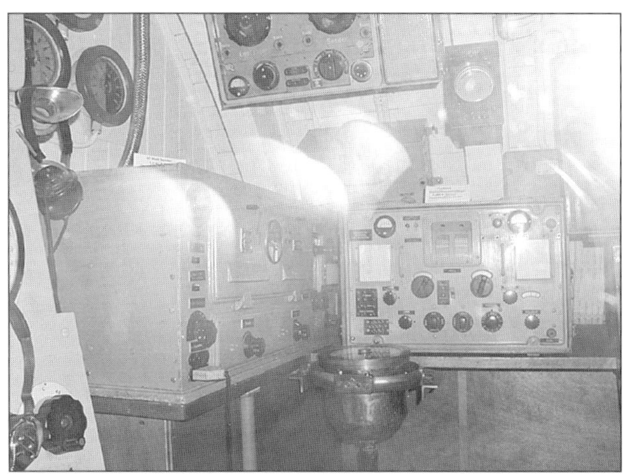

The submarine's sound detection room. When the sub was submerged, this is where tactical noise location took place. When pursued by an enemy destroyer firing depth charges, these sound detection devices were the only way of determining an evasion course. Because water transmits sound much better than air, it was also possible to locate unsighted convoys.

A view of the commander's quarters opposite the radio room. Although the commander enjoyed the luxury of his own room, it was small and only separated by a curtain.

View of the chief petty officers' sleeping area. The bunks are behind the lockers on the wall. There is not much room to climb in, so some agility was required.

The on-board toilet. A tiny room that had to suffice for up to 48 crew, since the second WC on board was used as a galley store. It was fitted out as a pump toilet and could only be used up to a depth of 30 metres. It is not shown in the photograph, but the on-board toilets were fitted with a ceramic bowl. This often got broken during an attack, which obviously did not help to improve the hygienic conditions.

Left: The boat's bow area. The photograph shows a spaciousness that never existed in practice. Before operations began reserve torpedoes were stored on the floor plates, reducing the size of the room to just above the first mattresses.For maintenance or reloading, the only way was to remove or fold up the bunks so as to move the torpedoes from the tubes with the loading rails. The ordinary seamen's quarters were located in the bow area; the bunks were shared by crew members on alternating watches.

The maiden voyage of the Krick VIIb, featured in the 04/2003 edition of the magazine 'Modell Werft'.

Left: The contents of the Krick Type VII construction kit, including propulsion system. Most components are vac-formed and need to be cut out. This is not a problem; it looks more difficult than it is.

Models of the Type VII Submarine

Model submarines of the VII series are some of the most popular submarines for model makers and many different construction designs exist.

Several hulls and kits are available for this submarine, together with a wide range of different plans. As a small selection, here is a brief description of four Type VII submarines.

The finished submarine. At the bottom the hull with the pressure resistant compartment for the RC components. Behind this the three covers and the diving tank mounted on top. The diving tank is designed to be open. It is filled by means of a pump and this causes the submarine to sink to approx. the middle of the conning tower. Diving is then achieved dynamically by forward motion. The final component, right at the back, is the upper deck.

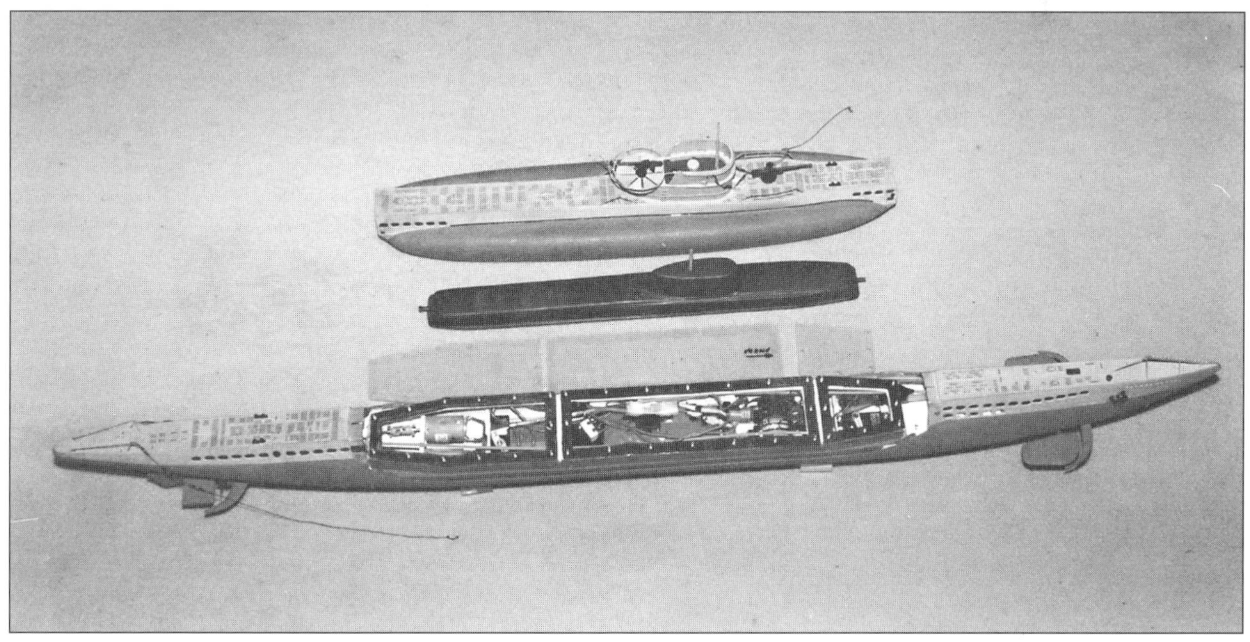

The robbe Type VII 'U 47'.

Krick Type VIIb

The most recent kit is supplied by Krick. They offer the Type VIIb model as a follow-on model to the Type Ia. The model is manufactured to a scale of 1:60. This makes it 112 mm long and it can easily fit in the boot of the car. It is 12.5 cm wide and 17 cm high. The kit is made of ABS. This appeals particularly to model makers who are new to model submarines and want to have a go at this great hobby.

There is a comprehensive construction and test report in the 04/2003 edition of the magazine MODELL WERFT.

The robbe 'U 47'

One company that for several years has had a Type VII to a scale of 1:40 is robbe. This submarine is 1.70 m long. Whilst it is one of the largest on the lake, it is nevertheless easy to transport, since it comes apart into two halves. Construction of the submarine's hull similarly uses vacformed ABS sections and is intended for the newcomer to model-making per se as well as anyone who has moved on to model submarines after making other models.

The submarine's hull is constructed in two parts. The submarine comes apart for transport and is only half as long. Clearly visible on the stern section is the equipment plate onto which all the RC and propulsion components are mounted. These components are located in a pressure tight tube, which is in turn mounted in the sub. The remainder of the hull is designed to be free flooding.

In the water the boat cuts an impressively elegant shape. Small details such as the crew on the bridge and fantasy flag bring the model to life (photo: Udo Schmidtke).

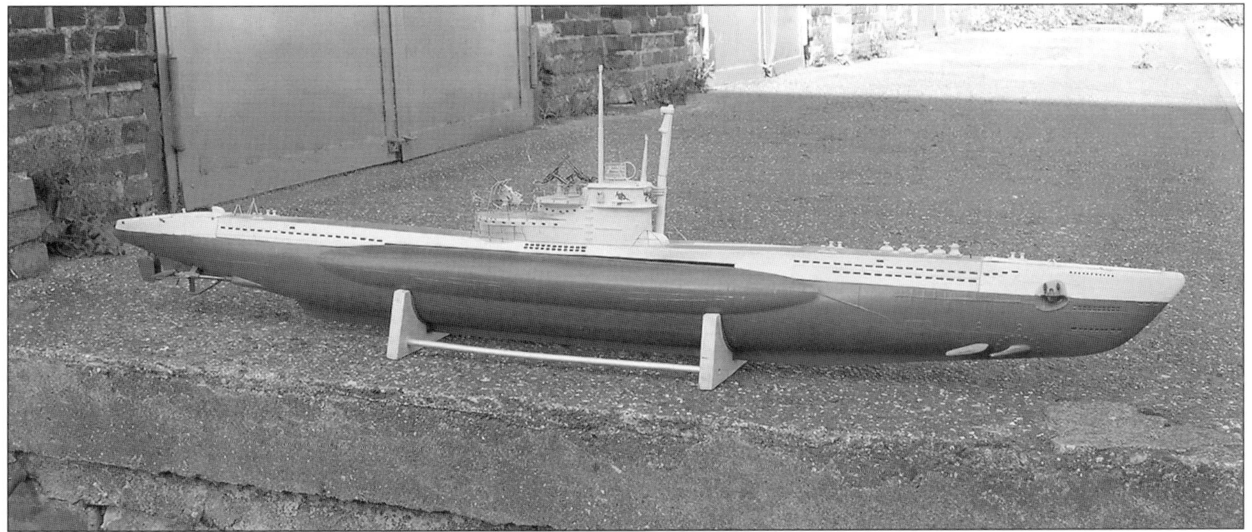

VIIc from Horst Hasse's Model Ship Building (photo: Horst Hasse).

It does not include complicated diving systems. The submarine dives dynamically through its own forward motion. It is true to say that the robbe submarine has developed its own fan base. Its size makes it well suited to conversion from dynamic diving to a pump-based diving system (static diving). In MODELL WERFT and the Internet there are construction reports and articles that deal with this conversion and provide assistance to those interested in this subject.

Bare shell of the conning tower and upper deck (photo: Horst Hasse).

Horst Hasse Model Ship Building's VIIc

These Type VII boats with GRP hulls and decks are in a different class, both in terms of price and quality. Horst Hasse Model Building in Hamburg is a supplier of such construction kits. The hulls are laminated by hand and are very detailed.

The quality throughout is very good, but in terms of the work required they appeal to the more experienced model maker.

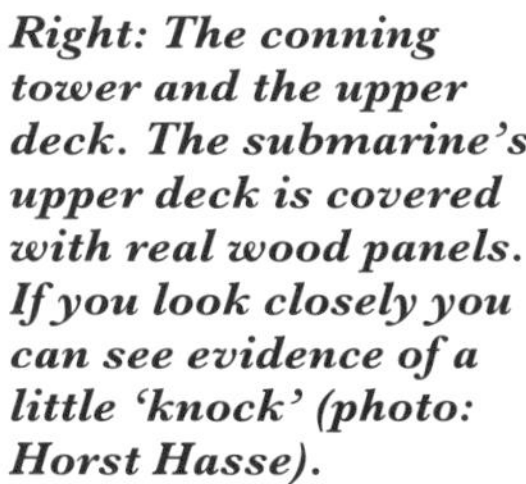

Right: The conning tower and the upper deck. The submarine's upper deck is covered with real wood panels. If you look closely you can see evidence of a little 'knock' (photo: Horst Hasse).

Scratch-built model of the VIIc

Jan Groot of the Netherlands put seven years work into his model. The model is totally submersible. Out of the water it becomes a very detailed diorama with much to discover.

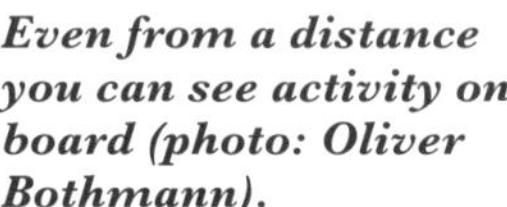

Even from a distance you can see activity on board (photo: Oliver Bothmann).

The bridge with the submarine's wintergarten. A type Focke Achgelis 330 Wagtail autogiro is just being put in place. The autogiro was dragged behind the boat and served as an additional lookout. When danger threatened – and the boat had to dive – the drag rope was cut and the pilot had to make an emergency splash down with his aircraft (photo: Oliver Bothmann).

Here a torpedo is just being stowed on the upper deck using a pulley. In the recess behind you can see the extendable snorkel (photo: Oliver Bothmann).

Everything must be stowed away properly (photo: Oliver Bothmann).

Submarine Type XXIII/240

The original

In 1941 the German Navy had only six small Type II submarines (called Einbäme – dugout canoes) remaining in front line service. These were designed for operation in coastal waters. Whilst other submarines of this type had been transferred to the Baltic Sea for training purposes, these six boats were designed to be used in coastal waters. They were stationed in the Black Sea, leaving operations around the British Isles to be undertaken by the larger Atlantic Type VII submarines.

This bottleneck resulted in a decision to develop a new coastal submarine, at the same time as developing the new Walter Type XVII submarine. One of the most important construction parameters was to make sure the boat could be transported by rail, so that it could be used both in the Mediterranean and the Black Sea.

It was intended for the submarines to be constructed in sections, which was then a new method. Having brought together the four prepared sections, the idea was for them to be welded together in eight weeks ready for the slipway. However, such was the prevailing situation at that time that it was no longer possible to manufacture or assemble the submarine sections at the suppliers, or to use the other facilities at shipyards in occupied France and Italy. Therefore it was decided in 1944 to hand over the construction programme for the submarines to the Germania shipyard. The intention was for all the sections to be built in Box 2 of the Kilian Bunker in Kiel and the assembly work to be carried out in the Konrad Bunker. This method was to complete ten submarines per month.

Of the 280 boats that were ordered as part of the con-

'U-Hai' after conversion work in 1961 on the Blohm and Voss shipyard in Hamburg. You can clearly see the front stabilisers along with the dive plane and the torpedo flap. Alterations were made to the platform for the underwater sound detector and the sound permeable bow tip of the M1 sonar fitted (photo: H. Ewerth archive).

In the bow area of the 'U-Hai'. Navigation, underwater sound detector, strategic operations and galley all located closely together. The two torpedo tubes can be seen at the back. The M1 sonar operator sits port side in front of the torpedo tubes (photo: H. Ewerth archive).

Top: The commissioning of the 'U-Hecht' on October 1st, 1957 (photo: H. Ewerth archive).

Left: 'U 2365', later to be renamed 'U-Hai' is raised on the cables of the salvage ship 'John Beckedorf' after lying on the sea bottom for more than eleven years (photo: H. Ewerth archive).

'U-Hai' and 'U-Hecht' with their new streamlined conning tower casing (photo: H. Ewerth archive).

A scale comparison. Two type XXIII submarines on the same course. The one at the front is to a scale of 1:30, the one behind to the scale of 1:32, as featured.

struction programme, 62 had been commissioned up to the end of the war, with another 33 units still in production.

The Type XXIII was a small boat. As a coastal submarine it displaced 233.86 t when surfaced (258.09 t submerged). The length of the boat at the keel water line was 34.68 m and the widest diameter 3 m.

The construction was new in so far as the shape of the hull was designed for sailing underwater. Proof of this was that it achieved a speed of 12.5 knots when submerged, which was higher than the 10 knots surfaced. Another exceptional feature was the very short dive time of only nine seconds and the long underwater endurance.

The boat was propelled via a shaft from a MWM 6 cylinder four-stroke RS 34S diesel engine developing 576 hp at 850 rev/minute. An AEG GU 4463/8 developing 580 HP at 850 revs/minute was used as an electric engine. The electric motor for cruising was a BBC type GCR 188 and it developed 35 HP at 300 revs/min.

The submarine was armed with two torpedo tubes that could only be loaded from the outside.

Space on the submarine was considerably restricted. The 17-man crew had only the bow area for living and sleeping and they shared this with the commander and his bunk or hammock. Unlike the larger submarine, it did not have separate sleeping quarters for the commander.

In 1956, with the Federal Navy in the process of rebuilding, the small, modern Type XXIII submarines were to be given a significant operational role. No more submarines of this type existed and almost all the submarines that had been scuttled had been raised and scrapped. Therefore the only course of action was to search for those remaining submarines whose whereabouts could not be explained and which had not been further damaged when they were scuttled. The Hamburg salvage firm 'Beckedorf' was hired to undertake this search and was able to pinpoint two well-preserved boats. In July 1956 in the Great Belt the 'U 2365' was brought to the surface after lying on the sea bottom for eleven years in over 50 metres of water. The 'U 2367' was located and raised in August, four miles south east of the Schleimünde lighthouse.

The submarines were brought to the Howald works in Kiel and within a year underwent a major overhaul. Other than fitting modern communication equipment and a type of sonar system not found in the Type XXIII, the equipment on the submarine remained the same.

After shipyard trials the 'U-Hai' (formerly – 'U 2365') was re-commissioned on August 15th 1957 and the 'U-Hecht' (formerly – 'U 2367') followed on October 1st, 1957.

Both submarines underwent several further refits. In 1961 they got a new streamlined bridge casing, which included soundproofing. In 1964 the shell was lengthened by 1.20 m to accommodate a similar diesel system to that of the new Class 201 submarines. This also required alterations to the ventilation and exhaust system. The exhaust gas mast was removed and the exhaust fumes were taken to outlet openings at the back of the conning tower. The diesel air mast was cut off above the connection to the snorkel mast. The snorkel shaft took over this function. This conversion led to the submarines being given the new type identification of 240.

The 'U-Hai' suffered a tragic fate. On September 14th 1966 the boat was sailing with two other U-boats and two escort ships of the Neustadt submarine training group to a fleet visit in Aberdeen when it found itself in a heavy storm. Due to a series of unfortunate circumstances the submarine

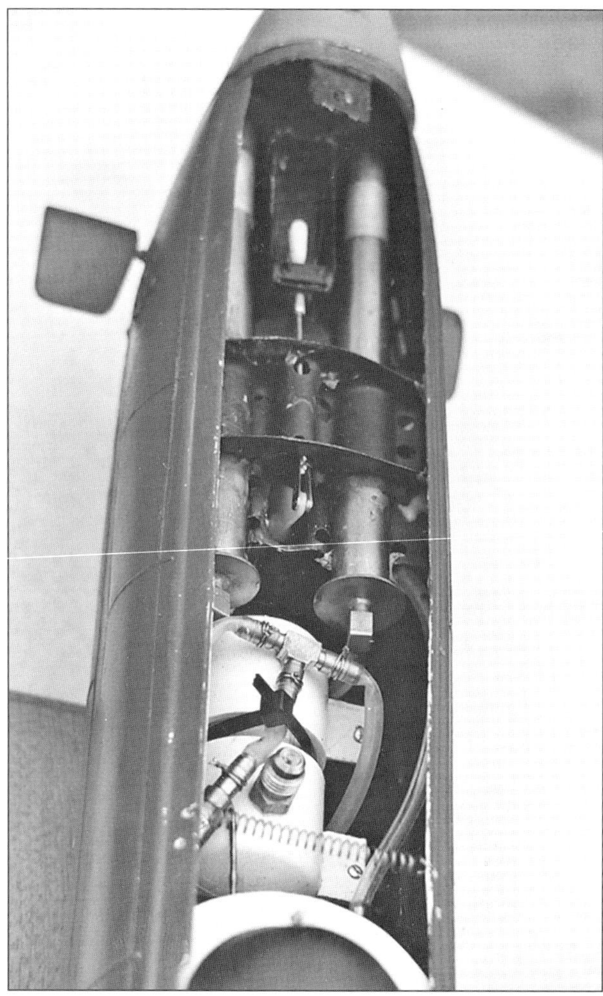

With a conversion kit the 32nd parallel type XXIII is also able to fire torpedoes. The torpedoes are powered by compressed air, which is fed into the mounting from a separate compressed air tank. The loading and closing as well as opening of the torpedo flaps are servo powered. However, when the torpedoes are fired they have to be collected up by hand and so it is advisable to think carefully before deciding where to use this show effect.

The attractive ageing effect can likewise be seen on the bow section.

The ageing of the model gives it an impressive level of detail. For example, here on the conning tower there are rust marks from draining water. Creating a realistic replica represents a real challenge for model makers. The bridge watch may be a touch small but it brings the model to life.

View of the hull of the Type XXIII. At the front in the bow the torpedo firing mechanism together with compressed air, auxiliary container; behind this, the pressure resistant compartment with the RC components and the propulsion motor. The cover to the right of the hull is secured by screws. Next to it, the servo-controlled compressed air, auxiliary containers of the diving tanks.

took on so much water that its buoyancy became unstable and it sank. In spite of the 'abandon ship' command being issued immediately, the submarine sank so quickly that only one member of the crew escaped and survived the accident.

On September 19th, 1966 the boat was raised from a depth of 47 metres and brought to Emden for investigation.

As a memorial to honour the victims of this accident, the 'U-Hai's bell was displayed in March 1973 in the consecration hall of the Naval Memorial in Laboe. There is also a memorial stone at the submarine fleet base in Eckernförde.

Two years later, on September 30th, 1968, the 'U-Hecht was taken out of service. Both submarines were later recycled for their scrap value. As a result of the tragic accident that befell the 'U-Hai', submarine design underwent many changes in order to improve safety.

Model of the U-Boat type XXIII

32nd Parallel, a company based in the USA and marketed by 'Harhaus Modeltechnik', has, as the name suggests, specialised in models to a scale of 1:32.

Unfortunately the company stopped production in 2002. The result is that their kits can only be obtained either second hand or in the form of individual components from remaining stocks. The range included a kit of the Type XXIII with a diving system based on compressed air. To a scale of 1:32 the Type XXIII is 1.009 mm long, 90 mm wide and weighs approx. 3.5 kg. The submarine's hull is made of polystyrene. The submarine shown here was made from this kit and belongs to SONAR member Gerritt Brammann, who has built it as an historical model.

View into the hull with the cover removed. In the middle you can see the fitted diving tank and the exhaust valve. In order to dive, the air present in the tank is expelled using a servo-mechanism and the boat sinks. To rise to the surface, compressed air is forced into the diving tank from the servo-controlled, reserve container and the model comes back to the surface. The diving and surfacing manoeuvres require a very well trimmed model and are dependent on the air available in the reserve containers. Airbrush reserve bottles are suitable to refill the system.

Chapter 4

Midget Submarines

Type XXVII 'Seehund' (127)

The Original

As World War II drew to a close a number of midget submarines were constructed internationally. Years later they were judged as 'acts of desperation' in the eyes of specialists. Many of the submarines were underdeveloped technically and their use resulted in the death of many crew.

The type Seehund was a real exception. Compared to the other German designs it proved itself to be the most effective and most advanced submarine.

The precursors to the Seehund were the types called Molch (Newt) and Biber (Beaver) and other designs such as the Neger/Marder (Negro/Marten) that were constructed more like a torpedo and were either not able to dive or certainly not with any great proficiency. Apart from the technical deficiencies of these machines, the fact that they only had a crew of one was also a big disadvantage.

The operator was very soon overwhelmed and on long operational missions was subject to considerable physical and psychological strain.

The 'Seehund' was designed as a two-man submarine. Alongside the commander, who also took control of steering the submarine, there was an engineer (lead engineer) who was principally responsible for operating the technical equipment.

The two seats were set one behind the other. The commander sat in front and if required could stand in the tower and steer the boat with his feet. There was also a second steering joystick in the lead engineer's seat.

The submarine was propelled by a LD 6 cylinder Büssing NAG diesel engine which developed 60 hp at 1,400 revs/min. This gave the submarine a maximum speed surfaced of 7.7 knots with an operational range of 270 nm. For underwater propulsion an AEG AW 77 engine was used that developed 25 hp at 1,040 revs/min.

Midget Type Seehund submarine exhibited in the Museum of Technology in Speyer (photo: Holger Oberste zu Freilinghaus).

Midget submarine of the Type 'Molch' exhibited at the Navy Base in Eckerförde.

Underwater the submarine achieved a maximum speed of 6 knots with a range of 19 nm. By reducing the speed to 3 knots, the operational range underwater increased to 63 nm. Both engines drove a shaft and a propeller with a diameter of 50 cm.

In the development of the 'Seehund' there were three different type rudder configurations. The first design incorporated a simple profile rudder. However, in practice this made the submarine's turning circle too big and so it was replaced by a kort-nozzle rudder. The results obtained were still unsatisfactory and so the third and final version saw the fitting of a two-blade rudder.

A view of the commander's seat in the 'Seehund', which is exhibited at the German Maritime Museum in Bremerhaven. On the joystick you can clearly see the stirrup with which the commander steered the boat with his feet when standing in the tower.

In contrast to the first midget submarine designs, the 'Seehund' had two diving and trim tanks. These enabled the submarine to be steered correctly at periscope depth. The operational diving depth was stated as 30 metres.

The submarine's main armament consisted of two Type G7e side-mounted torpedoes. When the torpedoes were fired, the submarine's trim tanks made sure that the submarine could be held at depth.

In contrast to the preceding designs, the crew were able to undertake underwater position findings with a simple crystal receiver. Radio receivers were also used on training submarines.

In spite of all the improvements, any mission undertaken with this type of submarine proved to be extremely hard work for the crew and there were occasions when submarines were lost precisely because the crew was exhausted.

At the end of World War II it was known in most cases where the larger submarines had sunk. If they could be reached, they were raised to the surface and scrapped to reclaim the value of the metal. However, in the case of the 'Seehund', many still lie today at the bottom of the North or Baltic Sea. A photograph on page 70 in the photo section illustrates what can be found on the sea bottom today, after lying there for decades, untouched and forgotten. The wreck of the 'Seehund' pictured has now been raised and is currently being restored.

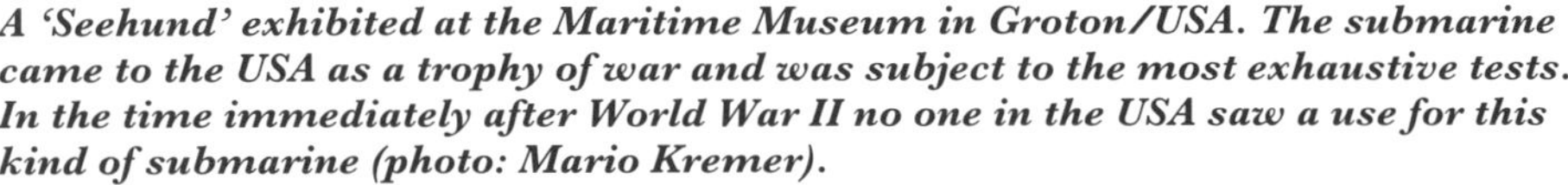

A 'Seehund' exhibited at the Maritime Museum in Groton/USA. The submarine came to the USA as a trophy of war and was subject to the most exhaustive tests. In the time immediately after World War II no one in the USA saw a use for this kind of submarine (photo: Mario Kremer).

Side view of the 'Seehund' built by SONAR member, Lutz Rahe. The relatively small size made it possible to use a submarine stand with carrying handles. It is designed so that the submarine remains secure even when transported by car. Many model makers have had a day when they have sailed the model at the lake with not even so much as a scratch, only for most damage to occur during transport. This angle clearly shows the detachable upper deck and the simulation of the welding seams. The conning tower hatch is made from a plastic hemisphere.

Aft view of the model. You can clearly see the kort nozzle and the torpedo mounts. The scale of the model and the resulting size of the torpedoes make it possible to fit the torpedoes with their own propulsion or to use them to locate additional batteries.

A view into the opened submarine. The GRP hull is sealed by a cover. As is clearly visible, this cover is tightly secured by four M5 nuts.

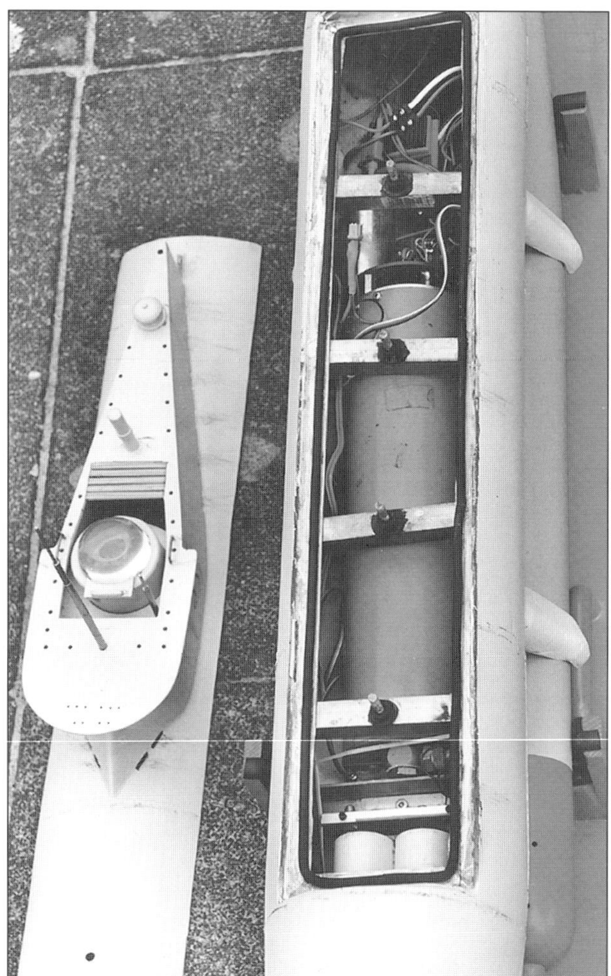

A 'Seehund' model submerged and cruising underwater. This submarine belongs to SONAR member Detlef Franke. It is similarly built to a scale of 1:10 and painted with a blotch camouflage. This shows how effective such a camouflage can be, it is extremely difficult to make out the submarine when viewed from a greater distance.

'Seehund' model.

Technical data	
Displacement	with armament 14.9 tons without armament 12.3 tons
Total length	10.39 m
Beam over torpedoes	1.684 m
Largest diameter of pressure hull	1,280 m

'Seehund' type XXVII in 1:10

A scale 1:10 model of the 'Seehund' midget submarine is almost 1.04 m long and weighs 18 kg, making it just about the right size to transport. Larger models are obviously also heavier. Models in the 40-60 kg class have a much more striking appearance, but you still have to lift them into and out of the water.

The submarine is fitted with a scratch-built piston tank. It has a volume of 750 ml and is operated by a diving tank switch available from 'Norbert Brüggen Modell U-Boot Spezialitäten'.

It is propelled by a Graupner Speed 600, which is supplied with a total of 4,000 mA by 10 NiCd cells via a speed controller. In addition to the drive function it also operates the dive plane as well as the rudder, which in this case is in the original's second design configuration.

The 'Biber' Midget Submarine

The original

The 'Biber' midget submarine was built in 1944 based on an idea from Lieutenant Commander Bartels. The prototype was christened 'Adam' and Director Bunte from the Flenderworks in Lübeck managed its construction.

The submarine was designed as a single-seater. Its armament consisted of two 53.3 cm assault torpedoes of the type G7e, which were fitted into recesses on the side of the submarine.

If required this submarine type could also carry mines instead of torpedoes.

The submarine was manufactured in three sections. These were joined together with bolts. The pressure hull was made of 3 mm think sheet steel and strengthened by several transverse bulkheads.

It could operate at a depth of 20 metres, although this could be exceeded by 50%. The submarine was 9.03 m long and 1.57 m wide and displaced 6.6 t. The internal width of the pressure hull measured 0.96 m.

The submarine's operator found the design to be very basic.

When sitting in the submarine his head would protrude into the tower. This was only 0.71 m wide and stood 0.52 m above the water level. He could see where he was going through three small glass windows in the tower. He also had a fixed, 1.50 m long periscope, which due to the space restrictions could only be used when travelling forward. A photo compass was attached to the outside of the submarine for navigation.

The design of the 'Biber' was based on that of an English midget submarine, the Wellman W 46, which was captured in Norway.

Those who operated this type of submarine in the Royal Navy considered it to be dangerous and unreliable.

When surfaced the 'Biber' was powered by a 2.5 6 cylinder Opel Blitz Otto Engine which developed 32 hp. With its tank filled with around 225 litres of petrol it had a range of 100 nm.

The 'Biber' with its side-mounted torpedoes. The submarine in the photograph can be visited at the Museum of Technology in Speyer. In Germany other 'Biber' submarines can be found in Potts Park in Munich and in the Motor Technica Museum in Bad Oeynhausen (photo: Holger Oberste zu Freilinghaus).

Its electric motor was a torpedo motor which developed 13 hp and which achieved a range of 8.6 nm at 5 knots under water.

The maximum possible speeds were 6.5 knots surfaced and 5.3 knots submerged. Both engines were connected to a single shaft and screw.

Dispute surrounded the use of an Otto Engine in the submarine. However since a suitable diesel engine was not available, no better solution could be found. The key drawback of the engine was the latent danger of the operator being subject to carbon monoxide poisoning and petrol fumes.

Whilst it was intended that the engine should be hermetically sealed in its compartment by a bulkhead, fumes often leaked into the driving compartment. The driving compartment had sufficient oxygen for 45 minutes and if a breathing device was used together with an oxygen bottle, this time could be extended to 20 hours.

A large number of submarines were later found where the operator had suffocated or died of carbon monoxide poisoning.

The submarine had only two diving tanks; control and trim tanks were not included. This design had the considerable disadvantage that the submarine needed to be trimmed with ballast before setting out.

When underway, the operator could only respond to any weight changes dynamically by adjusting the speed or part flooding the diving tanks.

The absence of trim and control tanks meant that it was impossible to sail at periscope height and the submarine had to surface before it could attack.

The operator of this submarine had to work under extreme strain. He alone was responsible for all the necessary steps required to drive and submerge the submarine.

Diving required the air to be evacuated from the two diving tanks in only seconds. At the same time he had to switch from the Otto engine to the electric motor, set the depth rudder and close the exhaust and ventilation valves. The lack of space and fresh air, poor visibility and the loneliness of long missions considerably increased the strain which the operator had to endure.

Another weakness of this submarine type was the firing mechanism for torpedoes. Reports cited many occasions when they went off unintentionally with dreadful consequences for both the submarine itself and any other submarine nearby.

A total of 324 'Biber' type submarines were made. Of these, the number lost was very high. Even though the 'Biber I' was rated quite highly, it was later replaced by 'Biber' types II and III with a two-man crew capable of achieving a greater dive depth and meeting the required range of 1,000 nm.

The type III was planned to include a diesel re-circulation system with liquid oxygen.

However, by the end of the war, these developments had not got further than the drawing board.

The 'Biber' surfaced. Since the hull of the submarine is very similar to that of a sailing boat, it forms a pointed wave shape extending backwards (photo: Lutz Rahe).

Above: This photo shows the submarine's slim profile. In the original the operator had to work in the tower in a space only 71 cm wide.

Above: A detailed photograph of the conning tower. You can see two of the three screw-fixed windows, while the periscope is located in the middle on top of the conning tower together with the inlet and outlet ventilation masts.

Below: A side view of the submarine. You can clearly see one of the two side-mounted torpedoes, together with the torpedo launch rail, which extends rearwards to the submarine's stern. The dive plane is located directly in line with the propeller stream. This makes for a very effective dive steering function. The submarine is sealed by a screw-fixed cover, located underneath the removable upper hull section.

One from the collection of favourite photos. At a depth of almost four metres the 'Biber' hovers over the pool bottom, captivating the observer with its unusual profile.

1:10 Model of the 'Biber' midget submarine

Like the model of the 'Seehund' it is possible to construct a model of this submarine in a scale of 1:10. The model is 90 cm long and 15.7 cm wide, making it very easy to transport. Weighing 9 kg it displaces little water and is likewise not particularly heavy.

The submarine featured here is fitted with a piston diving tank with a volume of 250 ml. It is controlled by a diving tank switch available from 'Norbert Brüggen Modell U-Boot Spezialitäten'.

Inside the 'Biber, space is at a premium. On the left you can see the propulsion motor. In front of this, the drive controller and receiver are set against the sidewalls. The piston diving tank is located at roughly the centre of the submarine and fitted with a Plexiglas pressure hull. Above the piston tank motor you can see one of two limit switches. These are actuated by the threaded spindle of the piston so as to avoid the motor continuing to run unnecessarily when the piston has reached its final position (fully flooded/fully emptied). The NiCd cells are located to the left and the right at the height of the piston diving tank (photo by Lutz Rahe).

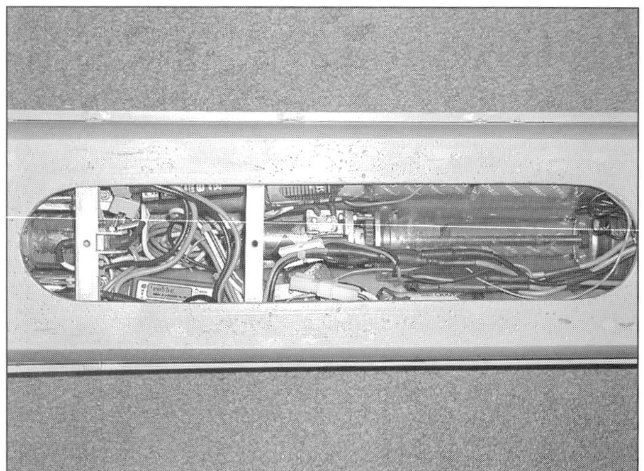

The 12 V drive motor gets its electrical current from 10 NiCd cells which have a capacity of 4,000 mA.

The submarine is steered by servos connected to the rudder and dive planes.

Delphin (Dolphin) Midget Submarine

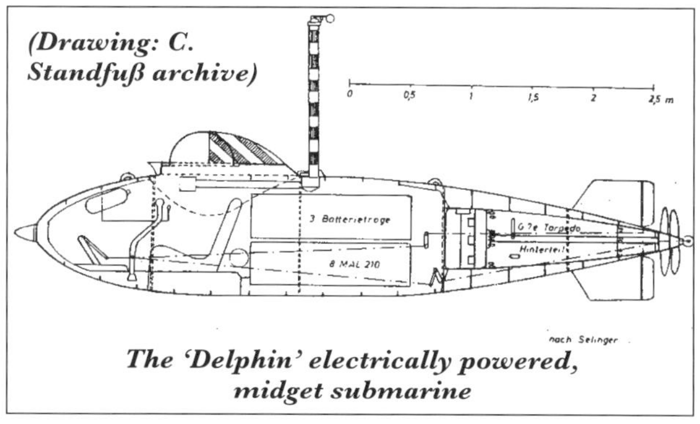

(Drawing: C. Standfuß archive)

The 'Delphin' electrically powered, midget submarine

The original

In 1944 it was decided that, in spite of their successes, the performance of the German midget submarines was unsatisfactory. Since the beginning of World War II several projects such as the 'Seehund' had been completed successfully. Nevertheless, while the single or two-man operation certainly had fundamental shortcomings, the performance limitations of the crew still have to be seen in terms of the problems associated with the submarine itself.

It was believed that one possible way of addressing these weaknesses would be to reduce the length of the missions. However, this contradicted the purpose of the existing submarines and therefore it was decided that the problem could only be solved by new designs.

The development work was accelerated. By the middle of 1944 several designs had been constructed as models and tested. One of these designs was the 'Delphin' (dolphin). The submarine was 5.48 m long, had a diameter of 1.00 m and displaced 2.66 t. It was envisaged that it would dive to a maximum operational depth of 20-30 metres.

The 'Delphin' on its stand. You can clearly see the snorkel behind the pilot dome (photo: Norbert Brüggen).

The submarine had a particularly streamlined form and the intention was to fit it out with an Otto re-circulation engine. New manufacturing methods using deep drawn sheet steel were to make it suitable for mass production.

However, the re-circulation engine was still in the development stage. As a result, the three prototypes built were fitted with complete stern sections of the G7e torpedo. The torpedo engine developed 13 hp and was fed by three battery troughs, located behind the pilot. In spite of this modest propulsion capacity, the submarine achieved an astonishing speed of over 18 knots on unarmed trials.

The submarine was designed so that it was easy to operate. The pilot sat right underneath the dome and steered the submarine using a joystick for the rudder and dive planes. The design did not envisage supplying breathing air to the whole internal space, so the pilot had to wear a breathing mask. When cruising at snorkel depth, steering of the rudder and dive planes was automatic. This was intended to relieve the pilot of some duties.

The submarine could only dive dynamically through the speed of its own forward motion. Consequently, the pilot was

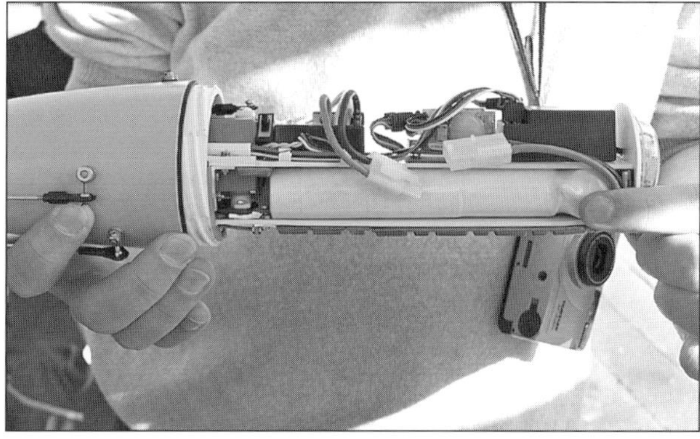
View of the RC component mounting frame. The drive battery is located underneath. On top are the speed controller, the pitch control unit and the receiver. The servos are fitted into the rear section. You can see the glands for the rudder lever-assembly on the outside of the stern section (photo: Norbert Brüggen).

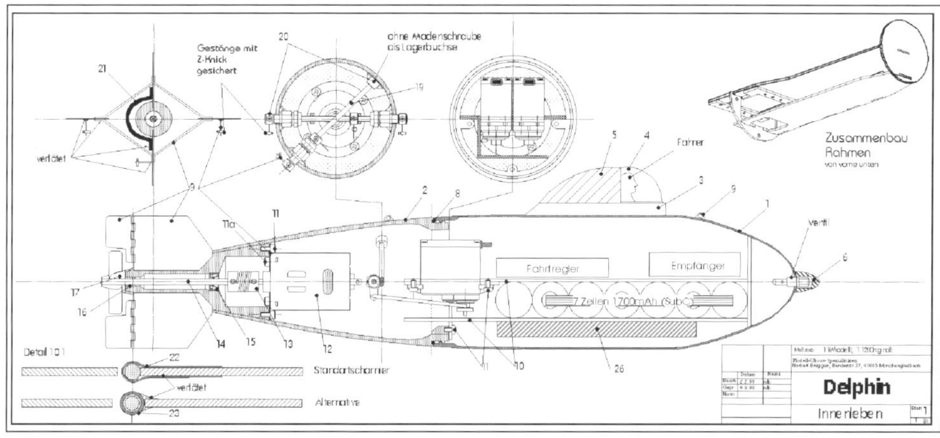

Sectional drawing of the 'Delphin' from the model kit (drawing: Norbert Brüggen).

left with only the trim tank to operate. A special reflector-compass was incorporated to provide orientation, together with a newly developed radio direction finder, designed to enhance the parameters for attack.

The 'Delphin' was indeed designed in accordance with new methods of attack. When torpedoes are attached to the side of a submarine, they drastically decrease its underwater performance. Therefore, the concept was to mount explosives and an impact detonator in the front of the submarine. In contrast to the Japanese kamikaze, the pilot should catapult himself out of the submarine before it hit. Bearing in mind the pilot's very small chance of survival after ejecting, the difference between this concept and that of a kamikaze remains tenuous, to say the least. In fact, tests ended up showing that it was not possible to get out of the submarine when travelling at full speed and so this plan was rejected.

Trials with a torpedo slung beneath the submarine's hull resulted in a considerable reduction in speed, down to 4-5 knots, so the attempt was made to solve the armament problem by carrying a mine. Again these trials failed to produce an acceptable result.

Apart from the three prototypes built, the 'Delphin' never really got past the trial stage. All three submarines were blown up on May 1st, 1945 in Pötenitz near Travemünde together with their design plans.

In 1945 a restored example of the 'Delphin' was exhibited in the USA in the context of presenting captured midget submarines. However, the Americans had no special interest in midget submarines and no one knows where this submarine ended up. Indeed, it is very probable that the last 'Delphin' still lies somewhere forgotten in a US Navy store.

The 'Delphin' to a scale of 1:12

The model of the 'Delphin' supplied by 'Norbert Brüggen Modell U-Boot Spezialitäten' is not a complicated construction. It is designed more with the enjoyment of driving the model in mind, rather than the time invested in building it.

To a scale of 1:12 it is 45 cm long and displaces 1.5 kg. The hull is made from GRP in two sections. It already has a moulded lock ring, eliminating the need for an additional bayonet lock.

The basic kit includes: the motor with watertight shaft assembly, CNC cut rudder blades, the dome assembly, all seals and rods as well as the installation frame and stand, supplied as CNC milled polystyrene sections.

For propulsion a standard 500-size motor is used, which enables the model to comfortably reach a true-to-scale speed of 9.9 km/h. It is possible to retrofit the model with a more powerful motor. In this case it is recommended to also fit a pitch control unit to improve the model's handling.

Like the original, the model dives purely dynamically and it is steered using the rudder and dive planes. The size of the hull is large enough to incorporate the RC components and also enable the installation of standard servos. The motor is supplied by seven cells and is regulated by a simple electronic speed controller with BEC system. The RC components are mounted onto a mounting frame and are easily accessible, when the large front section of the hull is detached.

The submarine is very agile and provides every encouragement for you to 'give it full throttle' underwater. At the same time, for anyone who is new to radio controlled models it is very forgiving in its handling. Whilst it may not be very true to the original, it is certainly quite spectacular to make the model 'Delphin' jump into the air at top speed.

Due to its compact size, you can always find space in the car for this submarine, even on holiday, while other submarines have to stay at home.

A touch of top speed air acrobatics (photo: Norbert Brüggen).

Chapter 5

The Submarine of Tomorrow

Experimental submarine USS 'Albacore' AGSS-569

The Original

If you look at the hull shape of submarines that were developed in World War II, it is evident that, apart from a few exceptions, they were designed with a form that was best suited to travelling on the surface. The reason for this is that the submarines of this time could only remain submerged for a limited period of time and would travel surfaced for most of their operational deployment.

At the beginning of the 1950s the US Navy looked at the development of experimental submarines with a hull shape that would meet all the hydrodynamic demands of a modern submarine with excellent underwater performance.

The USS 'Albacore' is the result of this development. The submarine's design represented a new developmental stage in minimising water resistance. The origins of this development are found, for example, in the German Type XXI submarines.

The 'Albacore' was propelled by two diesel engines, which supplied the charge for a 7,500 hp electric motor. It did not carry any armament. In the time that it was in service from 1955 to 1971 it was employed to carry out trials. Different rudder configurations were tested in order to determine the submarine's manoeuvrability. The given hull shape made the 'Albacore' the quickest submarine in the US Navy. Its highest recorded speed came in 1966 at over 30 knots. However, it is fair to say that the actual maximum speed was probably somewhat higher than this.

A museum submarine on a green field site: the 'Albacore' as it can be visited today in Portsmouth U.S.A. (photo: Norbert Brüggen).

Bow view of the 'Albacore'. The teardrop shaped hull was to become the precursor for all modern nuclear submarines (photo: Norbert Brüggen).

Other potential systems were also tested such as sonar, rescue and ballast systems. Indeed, this submarine contributed in no small measure to the development and safety of the US Navy's modern submarines.

After its active service the 'Albacore' was brought back to Portsmouth in 1984 and put on display as a museum submarine.

Technical data	
Length	205 feet, 6 inches.
Width	27 feet, 4 inches
Displacement surfaced	1,692 t
Complement	55 crew

U.S.S. 'Albacore' to a scale of 1:160

The scale of 1:160 provides the opportunity to take very large originals and make models that are reasonably easy to transport or alternatively, to take an original – although maybe not the size of a 'Typhoon Class' – and build a much smaller model.

When Carsten Haake from Bremerhaven built his 'Holland', he already proved that models to this scale are not just 'tubes that dive'. His second project likewise succeeds in reinforcing the same point.

Built to this scale his Mark I 'Albacore' is 45 cm long, weighs a total of 2 kg and is clearly one of the lightweights in the world of model submarines.

The 'Albacore's' GRP hull was created by first constructing the shape in wood and then using this as a mould. A scratch-built bayonet lock is incorporated in order to seal the hull.

It is possible to use a bayonet lock for all models that have a hull with an almost circular cross-section. The hull is easily

The actual level of performance provided by the X-rudder and double screw propulsion remains today still clouded in secrecy (photo: Norbert Brüggen).

The 'Albacore's' steering controls (photo: Norbert Brüggen).

detached just by turning it slightly. This avoids the often quite laborious alternative of screwing down a sealing cover plate. Indeed, according to the laws of physics, a bayonet lock is the solution that also gives the most effective pressure resistance.

The model does not have any diving tanks. It dives dynamically as a function of its speed. It is propelled by a 400-size electrical motor with six to eight 2,400 mA sub-C-cells. Like the original, the model has excellent hydrodynamic properties, making it very agile and quick. The underwater photograph shown gives an impression of this – you had to be really snappy with the camera.

The models streamlined shape gives you an idea just how quick it can move.

The 'Albacore' opened up. At the stern you can see the rear section of the bayonet lock. In front are the small servos for the rudder and dive planes. The receiver and BEC speed controller are located further forward. The batteries are arranged underneath the mounting plate. Assembly onto a mounting plate, as shown here, provides good access to all components.

The 'Albacore' is steered using the rudder and the stern dive planes. The dive planes mounted on the front of the hull have only a stabilising function and are not constructed to be adjustable.

Down and away!

The U15 S 194 out in the open sea (photo: J. Brume).

The Krick VIIb on its first trials (photo: C. Hofer).

Carsten Haake's 'Holland No.9' on a dive.

A 'Biber' in the Gosport Museum/GB (photo: A. Nied).

A model of the Type XXIII sailing at periscope depth (photo: P. Volk).

View out of the COMEX Remora (photo: Ingo Vollmer).

Olaf Hantke's model of the LULA.

The model of the U31 (Class 212a) on a dive.

Heading back to the top: a robbe model of the U47.

The model of the 'Stint' at a depth of four metres.

The Krick Type I in 'heavy seas'.

On its way to the deep. The LULA of the Reibhoff-Niggeler Foundation (Copyright FRN).

The model of the Jacqueline Tourist Submarine on a 'sightseeing tour' in the Waschmühle open-air pool in Kaiserslautern.

The U31 on trials in the Kiel Föhrde (copyright HDW AG).

The submerged model of the U15. The keel was later added, but cannot otherwise be seen.

A model of an 'Alpha' and a 'Typhoon Class' diving together.

A living piece of diving history: a model of the 'Brandtaucher'.

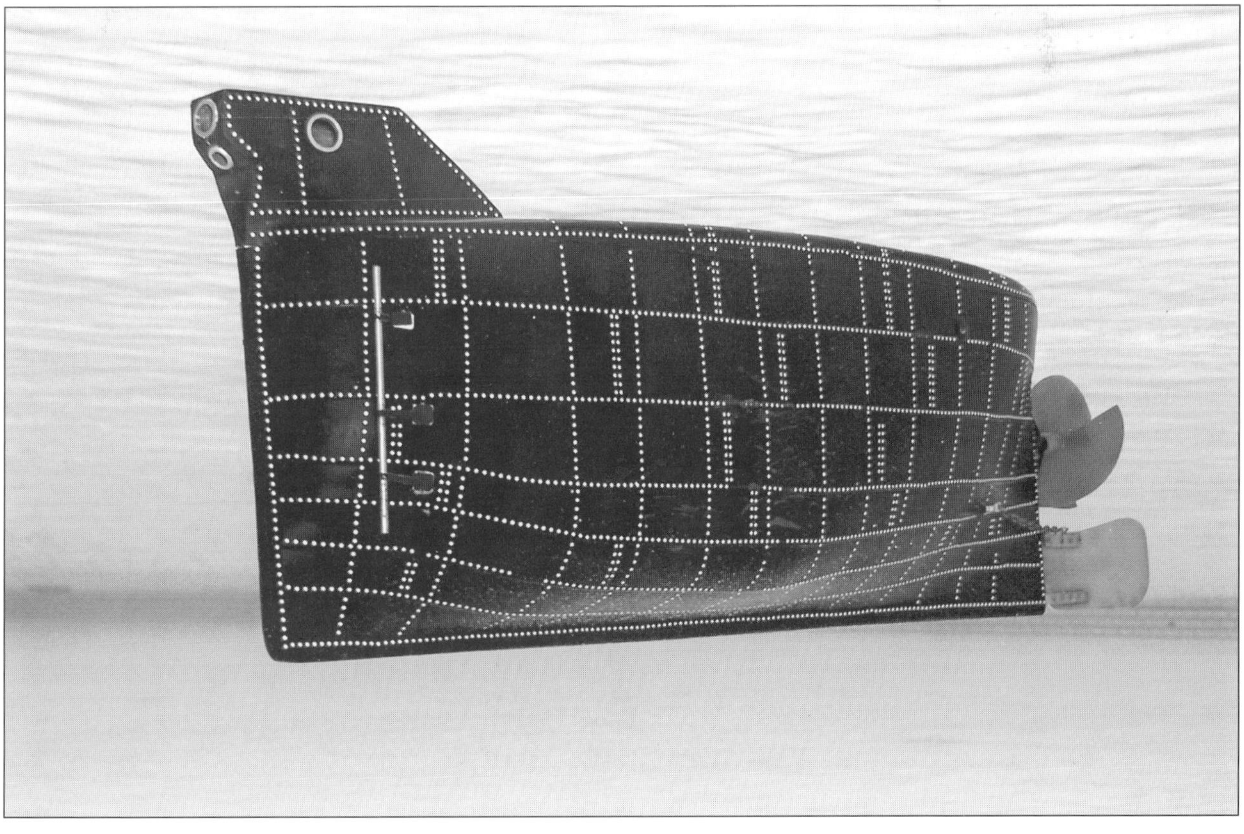

A work submarine of the type Mermaid V from Brucker Marine Technology. While the original is a fascinating vessel, making a model of it is a real challenge. Who will take the plunge?

Top: The 'Mermaid VI' rescue submarine of Bruckner Marine Technology all hooked up (photo: Jörg Haas/BMT archive).

Left: The 'Delta' research submarine submerges (photo: Delta Oceanographics).

Top: Bruker Marine Technology's 'Seahorse' on trials (photo: Jörg Haas/BMT archive).

Right: The author at work.

The 'Turtle' travelling on the surface (photo: Norbert Brüggen).

View through the bow window inside the 'Mermaid V'.

A Västergötland Class submarine of the Swedish Navy (copyright Kockums).

The wreck of a 'Seehund' on the bottom of the Baltic Sea (photo: Chris Hofner).

UREDD, a ULA Class submarine of the Norwegian Navy on a visit to Kiel.

The USS Connecticut; one of three of the most modern American hunter submarines of the 'Seawolf Class' (photo: Marco Kremer).

First attempts to dock the model of the URF rescue submarine.

The 'Shinkai' 6500 is one of the most modern deep sea submarines (photos: J. Greinert www.geomar.de/~jgreiner/).

Chapter 6

The Submarines Of The Federal German Navy

Class 202: 'U-Techel'/'U-Schürer' – the beginnings of the Federal Navy

The Original

The first submarines of the Federal Navy were two Type XXIII submarines that had been raised from the sea bottom and were later put into service as 'U-Hai' and 'U-Hecht' (see chapter III) and a Type XXI submarine, later christened 'Wilhelm Bauer'. These were assigned to the WTD 71 (Centre for Defence Technology) in Eckernförde.

The Type 202 was based on the Type 201. This was one of the first submarine types to be planned after World War II by the Lübeck Engineering Office (IKL) as project IK 6 for the new Federal German Navy.

In the initial stages of its development this submarine was planned as a hunter submarine. However, since it only displaced 100 tonnes, this provision was amended to that of a coastal submarine.

In 1958 the Federal Ministry of Defence issued a budget for a possible 6 submarines; this was followed in 1959 by the allocation of funds for another six.

Technical data	
Length	23.10 m
Width	3.40 m
Draught	2.70 m
Performance	350/350 hp
Speed	6/13 knots
Armament	two torpedo tubes
Complement	seven crew

Whilst this Type 202 submarine was being developed, work was undertaken to refit the Type 201. This later became the Class 205.

The Type 201 was a 350 t submarine. It was believed that, because of its size, it had a better chance of fulfilling NATO operational requirements. However, the submarines took too long to complete. Work to build the Type 202 was restricted, therefore, two units were used as experimental vessels to trial a super-size, active long-range sonar system, the like of which was not intended for the Type 201.

For test purposes the second submarine (U-Schürer) was intended to have a kort-nozzle instead of a blade-rudder. Although the contract for the construction of both submarines was raised in 1959, 'U-Techel' did not enter service until October 1965 with the tactical number S 172, followed by 'U-Schürer' with the tactical number S 173 in April 1966.

The submarines were named in honour of the Imperial Navy's chief submarine designer, Hans Techel and the head of the branch office for overall design and the main office for the construction of warships in the High Command of the German Navy, Friedrich Schürer.

From 1963 onwards it was discovered that the anti-magnetic steel that had been used suffered corrosion problems. This became one of the prime causes for the delays in construction.

Both submarines were constructed at the Atlas Works in Bremen. However, they were not in service for long, since

The 'U-Techel' experimental submarine when surfaced (H. Ewerth archive).

The 'Wilhelm Bauer', a modified World War II Class XXI submarine. Twelve years after it was scuttled, it was raised and brought into service as an experimental vessel. Today it is a museum submarine at the German Maritime Museum in Bremerhaven (H.Ewerth archive).

U1, Type 201. The Federal Navy's first new submarine. The Type 201 was preferred to the Type 202. After the construction of two experimental submarines, the development of the Type 202 was discontinued (H. Ewerth archive).

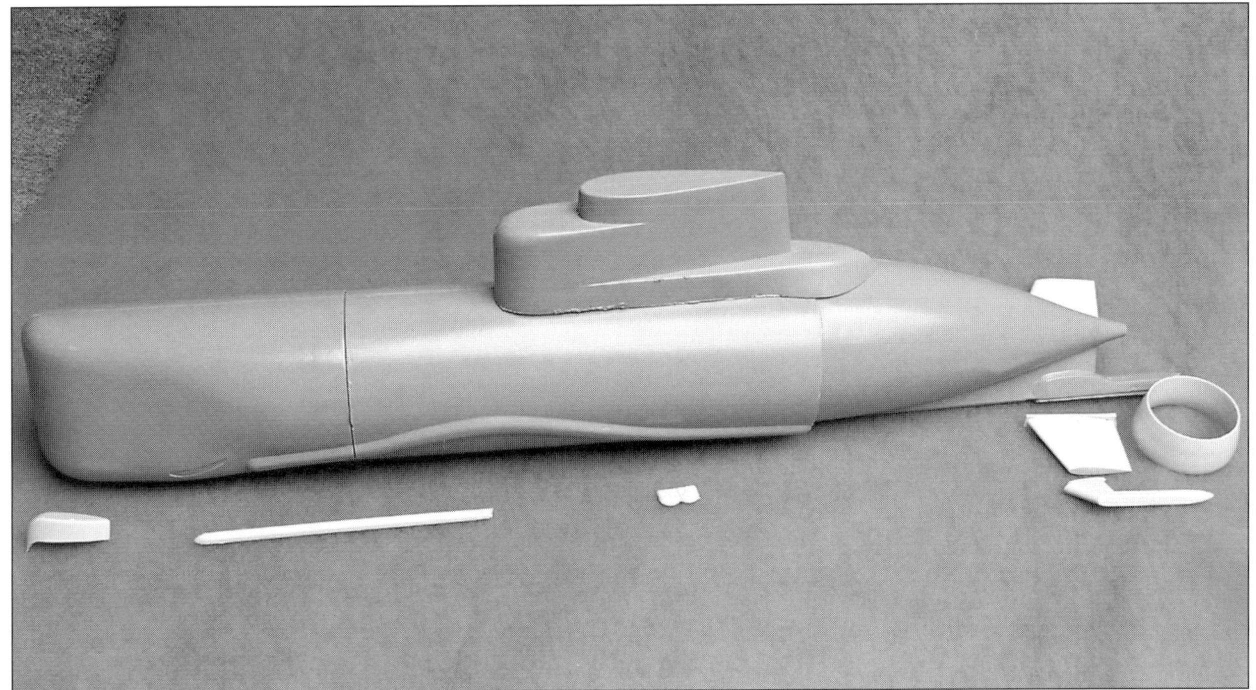

The individual components of the Type 202 kit (photo: Norbert Brüggen).

they proved unsuitable for the intended trial tasks. Due to a limited supply of air and a low battery capacity, it was impossible to approach the operational area submerged, and since the bridge was only one metre high, the sea would wash over it when the submarine was surfaced, even in a light swell.

The space limitations with a crew of seven also made it almost impossible to take test personnel on board.

These reasons and the major problems with corrosion resulted in a decision being taken to abandon their intended deployment on standard service after the trials. Indeed, 'U-Techel' and 'U-Schürer' were taken out of service just over one year later in December 1966.

In the history of IKL there was yet a third example of a Type 202.

The intention was to use this submarine to trial a new kind of 'Walter'-turbine system and it was given the project number IK13 with the modified class reference of 204. The submarine was of similar dimensions to the Project IK 6 Type 202, but its only power source was an electrical motor. The project was abandoned when its performance underwater proved to be unsatisfactory.

The 'Walter' propulsion system that was used in this submarine is now a museum piece at the German Maritime Museum in Bremerhaven.

The 202 in its element (photo: Christian Hamm).

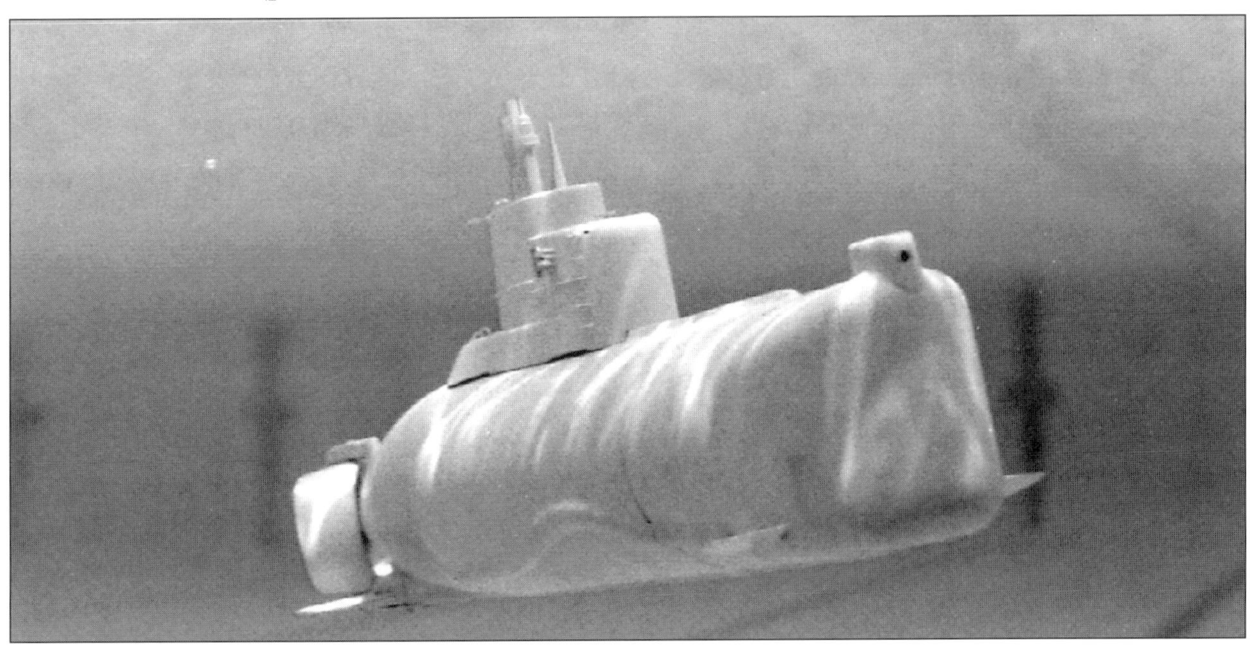

On the stand the submarine's unusual shape is apparent. Also, you can clearly see the dividing line of the bayonet lock.

Type 202 to a scale of 1:32

While the lack of size was a problem for the original, it is an advantage for the model. The Type 202, as supplied by 'Norbert Brüggen Modell-U-Boot-Spezialitäten' is an easy to handle model submarine whose shape is a bit out of the ordinary.

To a scale of 1:32 it is 722 mm long and, when equipped and ready to dive, it weighs approx. 4 kg. It is made from a three-section GRP hull. The kit also includes other components, rudders, fins as well as the kort-nozzle and sonar dome.

A reliable bayonet lock provides the seal between the stern and the hull. It has a diameter of 107 mm and can be purchased with the construction kit. All the drive and remote control components are mounted on an equipment frame, which is firmly secured to the stern and pushed into the bow section. A 500-size drive motor is located in the stern. A 20 watt motor is more than sufficient to achieve a scaled down speed of 4.3 km/h.

Detailed photograph of the conning tower showing the extendable equipment.

Anyone who would like to incorporate a suitable piston-tank but does not have his own lathe, can fit the submarine with a 500 ml Engel diving tank. However, this must be reduced to an internal volume of 200 ml. An alternative would be to incorporate a compressor pump system. Using the kort-nozzle as a rudder makes the submarine very agile. To achieve this same level of agility on the pitch axis, it is recommended to locate the 9.6 volt 2.8 Ah battery on a sliding plate controlled by a servo. The submarine is steered via the rear rudder and dive planes. It is similarly possible to incorporate front dive-planes, but these are not necessary to control the model.

Class 205: U11

The Original

Parallel to the development of the Class 202, as described previously, the Class 201 was redesigned and finally became the Class 205. The submarine was designed to be 419 tons in size. Whilst this was indeed greater than ratified in the Paris Contracts for the accession of Germany to the West European Union (WEU), which for the new German submarines had set a displacement upper limit of 350 tons, the increased size was necessary in order for the submarine to be operationally effective within the context of the alliance. Consequently, the construction of these submarines required the Federal Republic of Germany to submit a secondary application for approval.

The re-development of the Class 201 now gave the Federal Navy its first submarine. It was ideal for operation particularly in the German waters of the Baltic and North Sea where you often find shallow stretches.

In these waters there was not much point in deploying the 'swimming giants', in service with NATO partner, the USA and others. A high degree of agility was required as well as the ability to also operate effectively in water depths of only about 20 metres, providing a clearance of two metres of water under the keel. In addition to these special shallow water requirements, it was essential to ensure that it could operate in all seas within the context of the alliance.

Technical data	
Length	44.3 m
Displacement	surfaced 455.5 tons submerged 503.4 tons
Dive Depth	100 m
Propulsion	two six cylinder Daimler Benz diesel engines each developing 600 hp/440 KW and a SSW Electric Motor developing 1,500 hp/1,100 KW.
Performance	surfaced max. 10 knots/ submerged max. 17 knots
Armament	eight torpedo tubes
Complement	22 crew
Operational range	when cruising economically + battery charging: 3,948 nm at 4 knots.

With the introduction of the Class 206 submarines, the Class 205 submarines were successively withdrawn from service. One of the last submarines in active service is the U11. It is certainly the most unusual submarine of the German Federal Navy and also unique in an international context. The reason for this uniqueness is the refitting of the U11 into a torpedo target submarine. This was carried out in the summer of 1988 during its stay in the TNSW yard in Emden. A second steel jacket was welded around the existing external casing. This was filled with hard foam logs. After its conversion, the submarine was no longer very streamlined in shape, but able to present a real underwater target. In operational exercises the torpedoes are fired underneath the target and signal a hit electronically. However, since even the best maintained technology can develop faults and these can have dreadful consequences in the case of a submerged target, the main purpose of the conversion was safety.

In the Class 205 submarines the dive-plane configuration was one of the weak points, since the dive planes were each mounted left and right onto the rudder frame and, therefore, were not in the propeller stream. This made the submarines very cumbersome when travelling slowly on the surface or manoeuvring in a harbour. They required an extremely large turning circle. For this reason, in later new builds, such as the U11, the rudder was located in the middle behind the screw.

A brief tour around the U11:
The eight tube drains of the torpedo armament are located at the front of the bow. The photograph clearly shows tube II. The bags which hang to the left and right of the tube contain the rescue collars with diving goggles as well as a mouthpiece and hose for the emergency air supply. This system has connection points throughout the whole submarine; in an emergency it allows you to move from one connection point to another in the direction of the escape hatch. In the photo between the torpedo tubes is another mesh box. This is used as a store for provisions. Space is scarce on board submarines, requiring the use of every possible nook and cranny.

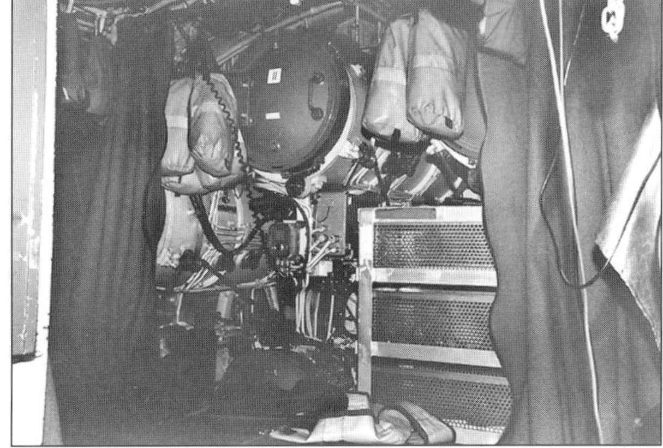

U11 'rafted up' next to a Class 206 submarine. Behind the staging you can see how the hull is thickened by the second external casing.

The submarine's conning tower. The two lights mounted above the service flag are not navigation lights. They are part of the submarine's alarm system. A prominent feature is the raised spray deflector at the top of the tower. The Type 205 submarines have the following extendable equipment: (from the front) periscope, radar warning aerial, radar slot-aerial and the snorkel. The top of the snorkel is the last device that appears on the photo. The fin running around the top of the tower is a part of the exhaust system. The photo shows retractable bollards, here in use aft on the first step under the tower as well as a pressure resistant container with the life raft.

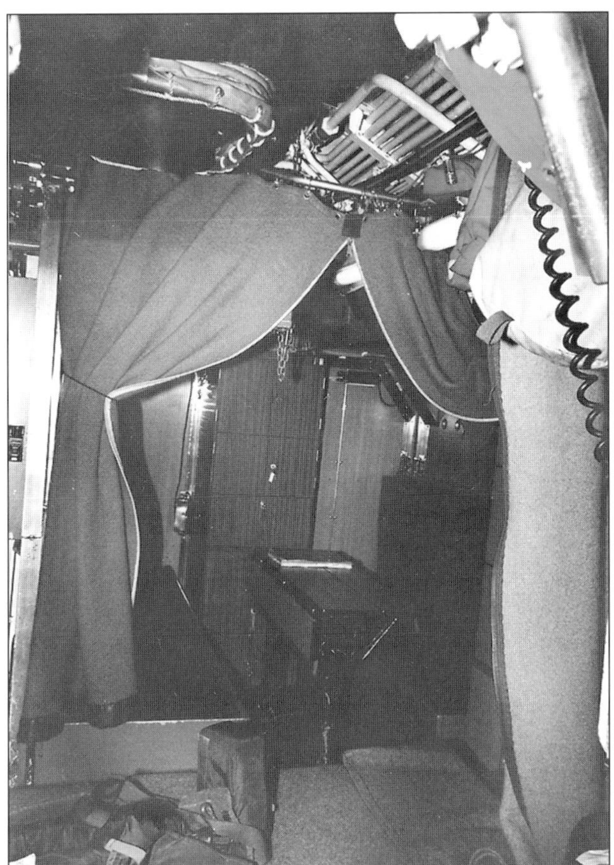

Left: The sleeping and living quarters of the senior petty officers are on the port side in front of the torpedo tubes. This room is only separated from the bow area by a curtain and contains five bunks. When not in use or during meal times, the upper bunks are folded down to make backrests. At the top left of the photo you can see the coaming skirt of the bow hatch.

Above: Located on the starboard side in front of the torpedo tubes is the passageway to the control room with the crew's bunks. Since there are only 14 bunks, some of them are used in a rotational system. The old submariner saying 'lying in someone else's fug' is only partially true in spite of the rotational system, since every crew member has his own sleeping bag. Foldaway tables in front of the bunks are used when eating meals.

Left: The galley adjoins the control room passageway. This is where the second most important person on board works – after the commander – the cook. On long missions food is the only thing that breaks the boredom and it had better be good. In a small area the cook has three hobs, a roasting device and a separate kettle. The photo does not show the back of the galley, where the sink and refrigerator are located.

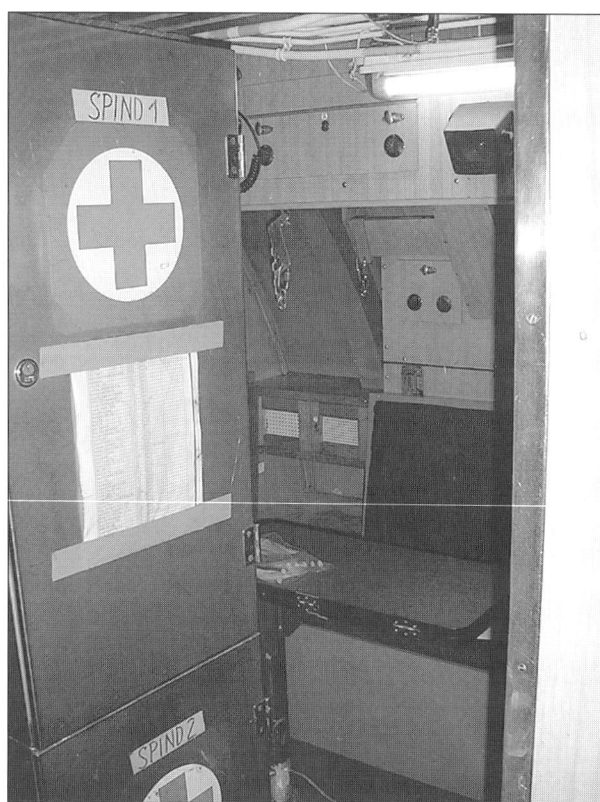

Top: The officers' mess. You can clearly see the wooden lockers on the wall. A crew member has not much more than a store cabinet to store his equipment (photo: crew of the U11).

Top: The steering controls are located port side opposite the fire control system and the plotter table. At the front of the photograph you can see the steering control for the rear dive plane, and just in front of it the control for the front dive plane. Between these two controls is the Papenberg, the display instrument (white in the picture) that takes its name from its inventor. On the display you can see a schematic illustration of the submarine's hull and the conning tower. Inside this instrument is a tube filled with a liquid; it precisely indicates the dive depth across the schematic illustration. The Papenberg is very important for holding the submarine at periscope or snorkel depth. The steering controls for the rear dive plane are next to those for the front plane. The front dive planes on the Class 205 are no longer fixed rigidly to the outside hull, as they were in previous designs. They are concave or convex-shaped half-hemispheres which protrude from the outer hull to produce the required rudder effect. The starboard plane has an upward function and the port side plane a downward function. This configuration is extremely quiet and particularly streamlined. Located above the controls for the front dive planes is one of the two central depth gauges. Next to the steering controls you can see the automatic depth steering and above it the magnetic compass. Forward of this, the last thing you can see is the rudder steering control. Above it there is another daughter compass and a display to indicate the shaft revolutions.

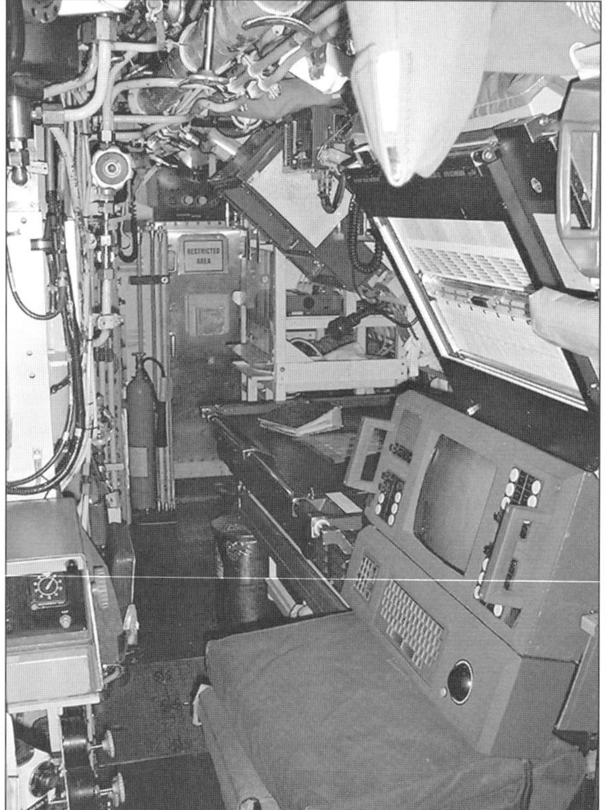

Left: The fire control system for the torpedo armament is installed on the port side behind the down-hatch. The helmsman's plotting and map table are behind. You can also see a door in the picture with the sign 'Restricted Area'. This leads to the radio and coding room. As the sign on the door indicates, no visitors and photos are permitted. On the left-hand side of the picture you can see the lower section with the extendable equipment. The stand-up periscope is likewise located here. In front of the fire control system is the commander's cabin. Only a curtain separates this from the central control room (photo: crew of the U11).

The companion hatch from the conning tower down into the submarine. The ladder is exactly the right size to allow one man to climb up or down. To avoid congestion in this area, when you are standing at the bottom, you should call out 'coming up' and 'coming down' when you are at the top. Around the edge of the photograph you can see the coaming skirt. This flexible tube extension can be let down and it enables escape from a partially flooded submarine (photo: crew of U11).

Behind the central control room you go further aftwards in the direction of the diesel engine room. There is just enough room to fit a WC in front of the bulkhead towards the diesel engine room on the port side, however you need to keep your head down. The main instrument panel for the submarine's central technical control room is located in the passageway to the diesel engine room and the drive switches are on the port side.

Behind the steering controls is the submarine's trim and deballast corner. This is the compartment where the submarine's upward and downward movement is controlled by taking on water as ballast or forcing compressed air into the diving and trim tanks. This is also where the trim i.e. the submarine's pitch is regulated. In the bottom of the picture you can see the main valves with vertical outlets and above these the corresponding exhaust, high-air and low-air manifolds.

The diesel room is the hottest place on the submarine. In the navy and on many other ships it is a tradition to give each diesel engine a name. Mostly they are women's names, since the diesels need to be looked after and cared for just like the good women at home. It is different on the U11. Here the diesels are called Cola and Sprite. Presumably these names were born of the desire for a suitably cold drink in such a hot room.

The drive controls. This is where the desired shaft revolutions and the operating mode are set. Above the wheel and the control lever, you can see three instrument displays that indicate the shaft revolutions and the armature current on the electric motor.

A view of the submarine's electric motor room and at the same time the last part of our brief submarine tour. You cannot see much of the electric motor other than the separately driven fans arranged in a 'v'. The motor is underneath these fans and is supported elastically. Above the motor in the middle of the photo there is a metal plate. Maintenance work is carried out by sliding along this plate. There is very little room in this compartment.

A U12 diving in the shallow waters of the Baltic Sea. The remote control system operates at 40 MHz. Since salt water does not conduct radio waves very well, the submarine's aerial is insulated. In this water it is, therefore, not possible for the submarine to dive below periscope depth.

A model of the Class 205 to a scale of 1:42.

Sonar member Peter Hauschildt has built a model of the Type 205 U12 to a scale of 1:42. To this scale the submarine is exactly one metre long, 10 cm wide, 17 cm high and weighs approx. 5 kg. Peter Hauschildt based the construction on the book and the planning folder 'From the Original to

At this point I say a big thank you to the crew and the commander of the U11, who allowed me to visit their submarine and stood by to provide explanations.

A U12 with the front section and the tower removed. You can see a part of the equipment frame and the diving tank in the middle section. As you can see, the submarine is certainly tight for space (photo: Peter Hauschildt).

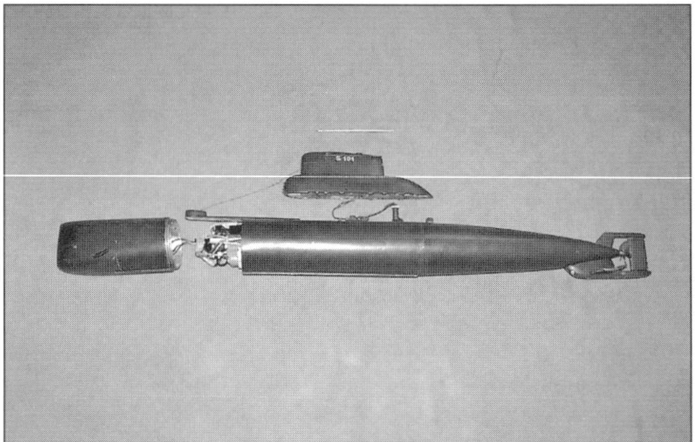

the Model: Submarine Class 205' by E. Rössler and H.J. Emsmann published by Bernard & Gräfe.

The core component of the hull is a copper tube, 10 cm in diameter. This was cut to the scale length of the central part of the hull. The stern, bow and tower were made of positive rigid foam moulds and laminated with epoxy. In order to provide better access to the hull, the central section has a ring lock on each end to attach the bow and stern sections.

The submarine is propelled by a Graupner 420 BB torque motor which drives a 5-blade brass propeller. Voltage is supplied by a 12 volt/3 amp NiMH battery.

The battery has a servo mechanism and is mounted on a sliding rail. As the battery moves backwards or forwards it shifts the submarine's centre of gravity, which causes the bow or stern to tip down. This mechanism makes it possible to change the angle of dive with minimum forward momentum and the submarine becomes more manoeuvrable.

The diving system consists of an Engel diving tank, reduced to 400 ml. The tank is operated using a diving tank switch supplied by 'Norbert Brüggen Modell-U-boot-Spezialitäten'. This switch likewise adds a potentiometer to the tank, which makes it possible to proportionally regulate the last centimetres of piston travel. This system only needs to be set once, at a point when the submarine is almost floating. Once this point has been set, every time the submarine dives down or rises, the dive tank piston always returns to this defined point. Driving the submarine forward when it is submerged is really straightforward since you do not have to keep on readjusting. The diving system is completed by a LTR-2 pitch control, likewise supplied by Norbert Brüggen, which can be switched off if not required.

Like the original, the model has both a stern dive plane and a spade-shaped bow dive plane. The latter can be extended or retracted depending on the effect required. To make handling easier they are linked to the stern dive planes.

Peter Hauschildt has also incorporated a cruise control in the transmitter. This mixer conversion makes it possible to select a speed on the potentiometer that the submarine maintains without the need to keep your finger on the joystick. Of course, this mixer has a manual override.

Class 206A

Diving with the U29

It is early morning in the Kranzfeld harbour on the Eckerförde submarine base. The firth still remains mostly hidden in the morning mist as, after the obligatory diving fitness examinations, I make my way to the U29. In front of the submarine on the pier, the commander of the U29, Lieutenant Commander Waldman welcomes me on board as a guest for the day.

There is still a little time before we set off and so he tells me a bit more about the U29's technical specification, a Type 206A submarine:

Technical data	
Complement	22 crew
Length	48.0 m
Width	4.60 m
Draught	4.00 m
Operational displacement	450 t
Speed	17 knots
Propulsion system	1,800 hp (diesel-electric)
Armament	eight torpedo tubes, sea-mine launch-system

The U29's coat of arms.

The author on the bridge of the U29. You can clearly see the nautical lighting behind and the extendable devices on the tower.

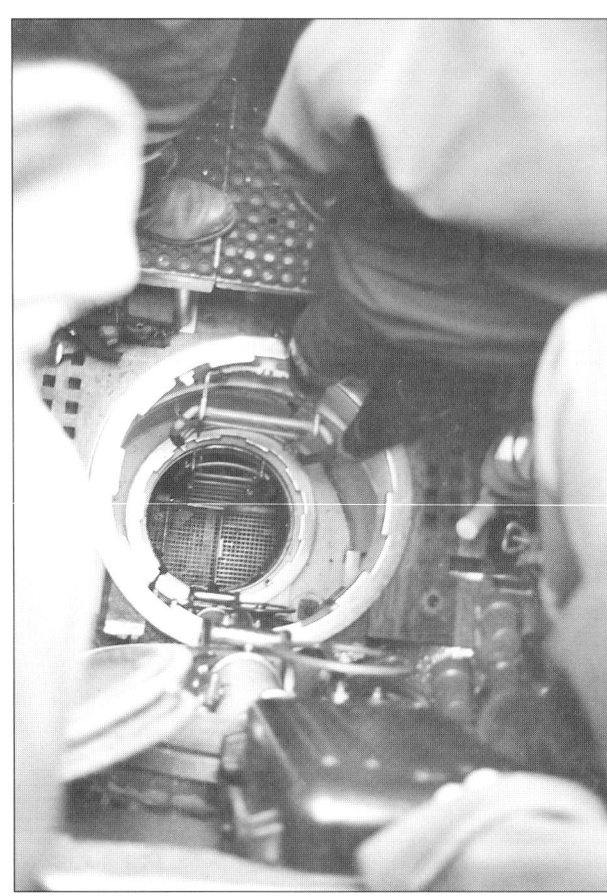

The access ladder viewed from the tower.

Practical training on the U29. Here the chief coxswain is instructing a student. In the right of the picture you can see the periscope and the snorkel.

Two of the four consoles in the operations control room. To save space the seats can be folded away. The submarine is surfaced, so the consoles are not manned.

Line up before casting off. The first watch officer briefs the crew.

The steering controls for the front and rear dive planes. The front dive planes are also spade-shaped, like on the Type 205, and can be extended as required.

The corridor to the electric drive-console. To the left and right of the corridor are the submarine's main instrument panels. The electrical engineer can be seen at the back of the picture. He is turning a hand-wheel to switch the machine's operating mode and set the revolutions per minute.

The water corner: a multitude of hand-wheels and valves used to trim the submarine and enable it to dive.

The submarine's rudder controls. The display shows that the rudder is in position zero, or straight. A compass is mounted above the steering console with which the helmsman holds course.

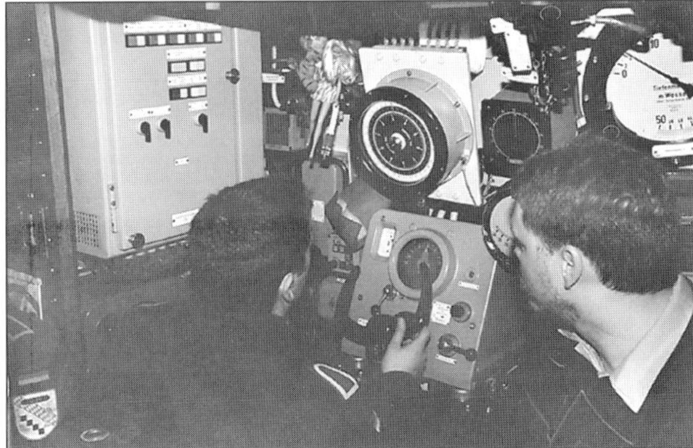

A view of the engine room. It is hot and cramped in here when the engines are running and with headroom of only 1.50 m there is hardly room to stretch out.

The corridor to the bow room with the crew's bunks. One bunk is folded up here to save space. This photo was taken during an exercise in which a casualty injured on the outside is brought into the submarine. At the back of the picture you can see the swimmer undertaking the mission in his neoprene suit and a crew member with the rescue rope.

When the sea is as flat as a millpond, the 'everyone abandon ship' manoeuvre is also much favoured by the smokers.

You access the hull of the submarine down the thirteen steps of a very narrow ladder. I first had to pass down my rucksack with the photo equipment because the entry hatch is very narrow indeed.

Once at the bottom I am welcomed by a pleasing warmth and the first watch officer, who greets me.

"Have a look round, feel free to ask questions, the cook's got a brew on, if you'd like a coffee." I discover that the cook is the second most important person on board after the commander. Morale on board rises and falls depending on what cook serves up. Later at lunch I was able discover for myself that what the cook manages to magic together in such a small kitchen is delicious beyond reproach.

The submarine's total length is 50 metres, but only 30 metres is easily accessible down narrow passageways and you soon learn to pull your stomach in. If you look at the submarine from the outside it looks even smaller, because more than half is under water.

The Type 206A is the smallest submarine in the NATO alliance, but it is precisely this characteristic that makes it so effective. It is very difficult to locate and extremely agile. No surprise, therefore, that these submarines are required all over the world for manoeuvres.

Creating a beautiful bow wave, the U29 makes its way towards the dive area.

I have a friend who is a submarine commander and he once put it differently, but succinctly when he said, "If we have to, we switch off all the motors and you cannot here a squeak out of us. You try doing that with the reactor's cold water pumps on a nuclear submarine!"

While all around preparations are being made to cast off, I have a look around. From the access ladder aftwards you enter the central operations room. In the middle of this room is a section of the cylinder containing extendable equipment and both periscopes.

On the starboard side is the chief coxswain's desk. This leads astern to the closed compartment belonging to the radio operator, who in submariner jargon is also called 'sparks'. Forward of the chief coxswain's desk and the radar console is the commander's cabin. Only a curtain separates it from the central operations room.

On the starboard side next to the access ladder is the submarine's wet unit, a small room, where you need to be pretty dexterous, even to take a shower. Adjoining this astern are four monitor consoles belonging to the central operations room.

After this you enter into the compartment with the drive controls. The ship's technical officer works here with his helmsmen and engineers; they ensure the trouble-free operation of the propulsion system and are responsible for the submarine's drive and dive manoeuvres. Steering consoles for the rudder and the front and rear dive planes are located in this room, as well as, further aftwards, the drive controls for the electric motor.

Three crew are required to steer the submarine; one for each of the bow and stern dive planes and then the rudder helmsman. The flood and trim valves are also found in this section. Without these the submarine could not dive. In submariner jargon this part of the submarine is referred to as the 'water corner'.

Moving further astern you enter into the diesel engine room and after that comes the electric motor. The diesel engine room also has the submarine's only bulkhead. When sailing in warmer waters the temperature in the engine room can be as high as 50°C. It provides only 1.5 m of headroom and so there are no prizes for guessing why there are two large cushions attached to the ceiling with yellow tape.

Serving on the submarine is not exactly for the faint-hearted. Having said that, the work is interesting and exciting and that cannot be said of many other jobs. If you want to commit yourself to submarine life, you must be very healthy and fit and be able to adapt to a close-knit team with the loss of accustomed privacy.

Forget all the drama you have seen in famous films; what is important here is total professionalism, your every action counts.

Space on board is tight. Apart from the commander and the cook everyone shares a bunk with another comrade. Demands are high; not only is movement restricted, but your work is divided into four-hour watches. After a few days at sea, it is hardly possible for the crew to retain a sense of night and day.

Exercises – so-called 'role-acting' – are used to mitigate the monotony of life at sea. These involve simulations of all possible situations that may occur on board.

Whether the submarine is on fire, taking on water or a sick crew member needs rescuing, the continual practice of dealing with crisis situations provides security and the ability to stay in control, even in an emergency when you have to act blind in darkness.

It turns a group of people into a strong team and anyone who has once experienced this way of working together will understand why in submariner circles you tend to speak of a family.

In the meantime the U29 has cast off and pulled out of the port of Kranzfeld astern. With its diesel engines humming quietly as they charge the accumulators, it travels out into the bay of Eckernförd. My question "man on the bridge?" is answered with a "yes" from above and with a "coming-up" I climb up the ladder. The 'Old One', as the commander on a submarine is respectfully called, is standing on the bridge and offers me a seat on the 'bridge sofa'. This is a narrow wooden seat covered in material; it is placed up at the far end of the bridge and enables two crew to sit down. The space at the front of the bridge is very tight indeed, since the entry hatch is in the middle.

The sun has now fought its way through the mist and with a beautiful bow wave the U29 forces its way further out into the firth.

I find out that the U29 is currently on an exercise lasting several days and that it only put back to port to pick up its guest, me.

It is only possible for submarines to dive in particular designated areas of the Baltic Sea and so it will take quite a while before we reach the area where we can dive. More than enough time to stay up here and feel the wind in my face.

"Everyone down the hatch, prepare to dive!" Back down the ladder; the flagpole, the 'bridge sofa' and the little mast with the nautical lighting are all passed down and the commander closes the conning tower hatch after the last man.

The diesel engines are stopped and following the announcement "hatch closed", the commander gives the order "flood the tanks to periscope depth." The word 'flood' is repeated by everyone and the U29 gently inclines downwards.

You feel a light pressure in your ears and the submarine is suddenly very quiet. All you can hear is a quiet whirring of the electrical motors and a clicking that comes from the periscope being moved. The first watch officer now stands at the periscope and compares the situation above the water with the data provided by the sonar and radar station in the central operations centre.

The diving area is free and after the commander orders "down to 40 metres" the submarine inclines again and the technical officer and his crew level it off at the ordered depth. In the central operations room there is concentrated activity and I go further forward past the officers' mess and the galley to have a look in the front of the submarine. Immediately after the galley there are the bunks for the crew. They are on the port side of the passageway and, as required, can be folded up or down. In the middle there are tables, since this area is used for sleeping, eating and for spending time off-watch.

Nets are attached to the ceiling of the passageway containing food provisions. There is little space on a submarine and so every nook and cranny is used.

When I get to the bow, I find the submarine's eight torpedo tubes, separated from the bow room by a curtain. The torpedoes are wire-guided.

Having come to the end of my tour, I end up in the officers' mess enjoying a fine lunch with Lieutenant Commander Waldmann. He explains to me the advantages of wire-guidance. It enables torpedoes to be guided to their target over very long distances. To my question: "How far?" he just winks at me and answers "a very long way." Even submariners like to have their secrets.

After lunch I am back in the central operations room and have the chance to sit at the first watch-officer's monitor console.

This is where all the technical reconnaissance information is brought together, enabling the first watch officer to provide the commander with a report as to the situation above water and to work with the crew to calculate measures or key strategies in the case of potential attack.

The sonar operator gives me a brief introduction into the operation of the consoles and I am impressed by how much information is processed. When the submarine is submerged it relies on only one sensor and hardly produces a sound. The infamous 'ping' of an active echolocation is hardly ever used since it would immediately reveal the presence of a submarine to a potential enemy.

Sounds that emanate from other vessels can be located over very large distances. The technology enables the operator to exactly attribute these sounds to individual ships. A trackball on the console enables me to listen for 360° all around the submarine and I am amazed how loud it is underwater.

You can clearly hear the sound made by screws and engines and also the rattle of the nets laid out by fishing smacks. Yet the sound of the submarine's own screw is fleetingly quiet.

Without a point of reference it is sometimes difficult at distance to tell the difference between a model and the original. Here is the U15 on the high seas of the Ihlow Sea in Aurich.

We have been submerged for several hours and now, around me, preparations are underway to end this dive to return to the surface. The submarine rises to the surface like a lift and the conning tower hatch is opened. Nevertheless, there is no rest yet for the current watch. The commander orders an exercise where a member of the crew who has been injured on the outside has to be brought back down from the conning tower and into the submarine. A rescuer belt is fitted under the arms of the 'injured party' and he is carefully lowered down through the access hatch. This may sound quite easy, but it is actually made particularly difficult by the lack of space in the hatch. Below, other crew members are already waiting to give him medical first aid and to carry him into the bow room. When he gets there, he is wrapped in an insulating blanket and treated by the medical orderly, the crew member have undergone the respective additional training.

The exercise was a success and the next exercise, "everyone abandon ship" can almost be seen as the commander's thank you, since, when outside, the smokers finally get their reward.

The U29 is now heading home on course for Eckernförde. I am sitting up on the 'bridge sofa' again and talking to the commander and the first watch officer.

Like all the other members of the crew they are passionate about their job and also proud, because jobs like this are few and far between. The willingness to do such a job and the satisfaction to be gained from it exemplifies that subtle distinction between a profession and a calling.

A short time later and we are back in port and the guest is bid farewell with a return-to-port Coca-cola.

The U29 needs to get back to sea again quickly since the multi-day exercise is far from over. It would have been good to go with them.

A big thank you to the then commander of the submarine flotilla, Captain at Sea, Eberbach for giving me the chance to take this tour and write the article, as well as the commander and crew of the U29, who provided me with a fascinating insight into their work.

Type 206 A to a scale of 1:35

Submarine models are similarly a matter of personal taste. If you find that you like the unusual shape of the Type 206 A, then Engel Modelbau gives you the opportunity to build a beautiful model. However, some experience of model making is necessary, since the model kit is not exactly designed for complete beginners. To a scale of 1:35 the model is 1.50 metres long and 14.7 cm wide. Surfaced, it displaces 13.8 kg and submerged, 14.7 kg.

The GRP hull consists of an upper and lower shell. The pressure hull is sealed by an aluminium cover; this is screwed onto the opening on the laminated intermediate deck of the lower half of the hull. The upper section of the deck and the conning tower are designed to be free flooding. This enables the incorporation of two short Engel tanks with a total volume of one litre into the very small internal space in the lower half of the hull.

The standard propulsion is a geared, size 540 motor. It is powered by the 6 volt, 10 Ah lead acid gell cell main battery. This propulsion gives the submarine a speed of 5.6 km/h, appropriate in scale to that of the original.

Any model maker that uses this submarine to convert from dynamic to static diving has the opportunity of making the submarine submerge section by section. It is recommended not to simply fully flood the tanks, but to start by flooding one part and seeing how the submarine performs. Driving a submarine using diving tanks has the advantage that, if the submarine is well trimmed, it is possible to hold it almost still underwater.

It is a fact that many model builders never really get around to finishing their submarines. Such is the way that this great hobby develops, that you are always looking to improve or modify a model. Consequently, it is good when you have a model that offers you this freedom. This is what happened to the author and his model of the 206A.

It began with the modification to a sickle-shaped propeller to match the original. Once the propeller had been shortened and the model was in the water for the first time, it quickly became apparent that the standard 540 motor was no longer

A few hundred metres away from the original, the U15 has surfaced in the diver training hall on the Eckernförde submarine base.

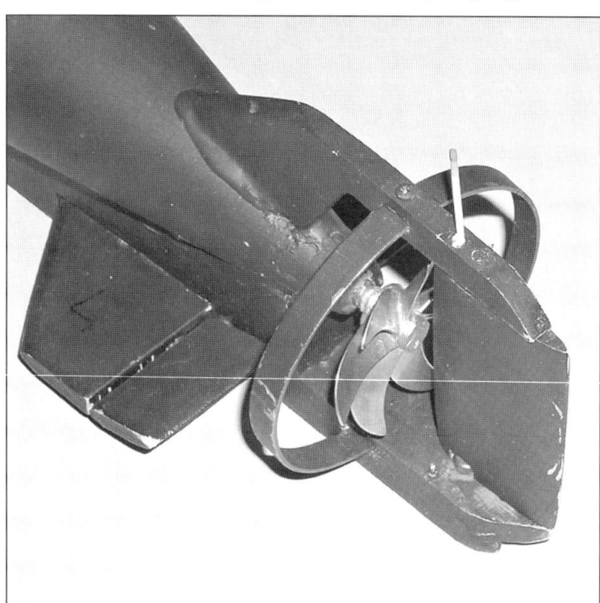

The stern with the adapted sickle-shaped propeller.

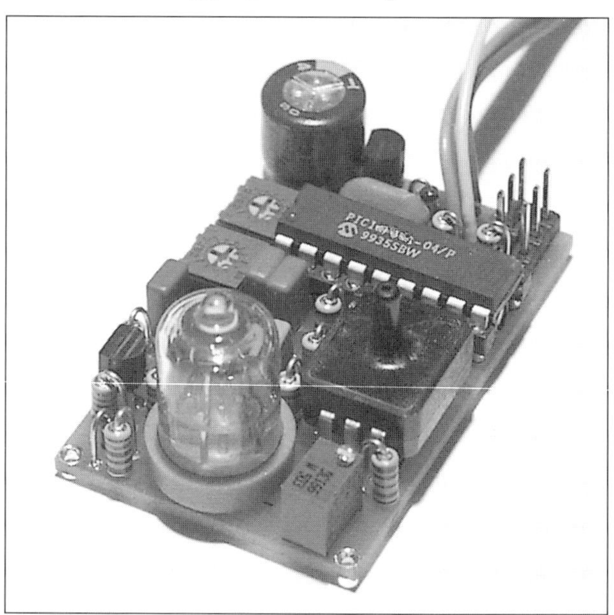

The Norbert Brüggen pitch and depth controller.

The two light diodes set into the upper part of the conning tower; the front one has a polished socket, the one behind was inserted without a socket into a hole in the conning tower.

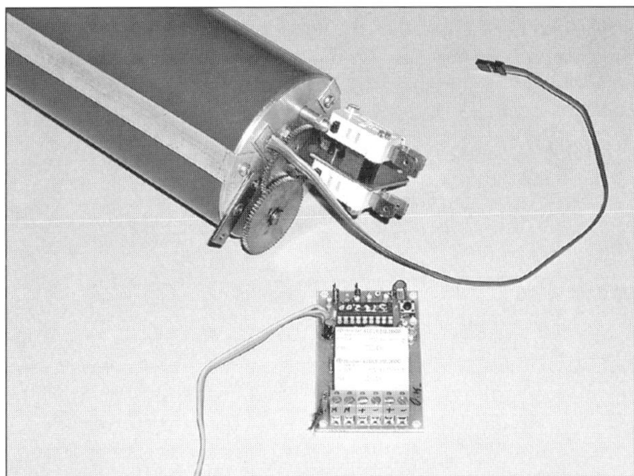

One of the dive pumps with its fully proportional controller.

powerful enough to adequately turn the propeller, greatly reducing the model's performance. Help came in the form of a Hopf Viper 650 XL motor; this was entirely compatible with the existing gear system and therefore avoided a total rebuild of the propulsion system.

The construction kit was already a few years old. It came with a switch plate to regulate the diving tanks. Whilst this worked brilliantly once all cables were tightly secured, it did take up a lot of space in the already tight-fitting hull. As a result, this component was replaced by a higher specification electronic diving tank switch from 'Brüggen'. The fact that it took up less space was not the only factor in choosing this switch. The 'fail-safe' safety functions and the under voltage recognition were also decisive. In the case of reception difficulties or when the batteries get too low, it switches the tanks to deballast, so to avoid losing the submarine or forcing the captain to take a cold bath.

Original and Model.

Another sensible addition involved the incorporation of a pitch/depth controller. The way a submerged submarine travels underwater depends on the hydrodynamic properties of the hull shape. Some modern submarines are designed to operate entirely underwater. They have fewer problems, since, when submerged, the hull's shape dictates that it is for the most part neutral.

Older submarine types such as a VIIc, for example, have a hull that is shaped very much like a surface ship. This shape means that as the water streams from the bow against the hull it is forced upwards and, as the submarine travels forward, it has a tendency to rise up. As a consequence the captain must continually seek to readjust and, rather than travel flat in the water, the submarine travels more dolphin-style. An inclinometer in the pitch controller picks up any tendency of this happening and automatically steers the submarine to an even keel using the dive planes. This makes it much easier to drive the submarine and it also looks better.

The depth controller is an electronic switch. In combination with the pressure sensor, it enables the captain to use the transmitter joystick to steer the submarine to a pre-defined depth and to hold it there. 'Norbert Brüggen Modell-U-Boot-Spezialitäten' offers a range of reliable pitch/depth controllers.

Another modification to the submarine was the result of a problem involving the semi-circular cast iron keel. Instead of being permanently fixed into the submarine, it had to be tilted up time and time again in order to change the batteries. The result was that the submarine was often tilted at an angle in the water. In submarines of the same type this problem has been solved by replacing the internal keel with a keel screwed to the outer underside of the submarine.

This not only freed up more space in the submarine, but it also significantly lowered the submarine's centre of gravity.

There is no doubt that this does have a detrimental effect on the submarine's appearance. Nevertheless, when the submarine is in the water, you cannot see the keel, unless you happen to have your diving gear on and are swimming underneath it.

On its stand the submarine's keel is kept hidden by a label with the U 15 S 194's original coat of arms and the technical data relating to the model.

In fact, the low centre of gravity proved to be singularly beneficial for further modifications, such as the option of fitting a different conning tower mechanism. Even with all equipment extended, the submarine does not lean when sailing in a curve.

Whilst the model was still 'not quite finished' there followed two other modifications. The submarine was often in the water and slowly became a kind of creative building site, a workhorse, which looked as if it had seen better days. Like many of my model-making colleagues who are always trying out new things, I would beg the purists' forgiveness and state my intention of returning the outside to its proper glory, once all the improvements and modifications were complete. Having said that, you have to remember that the originals are at sea almost every day and also do not always look their best.

A further modification involved the lighting. Up until then the submarine was equipped with only steaming and side navigation lights. Consequently, night sailing was not much fun since you could hardly see a thing. There is something special about meeting up at night to sail submarines, even if it just happens by chance when you stay on after it gets dark. These

A side/bow view of the Narwal. On the top at the front you can just make out the grid cover of the front vertical propulsion (photo: Detlef Franke).

meets usually take place at outdoor swimming pools. The beautiful underwater illuminations begin just after dusk. Creativity knows almost no bounds. The pool is lit up by underwater searchlights or the sparkle and flash of dozens of light diodes, fitted almost invisibly into the submarines. The diodes used have such a strong light intensity that it only requires five of these small components at a distance of four metres to flood the pool bottom with a 2 metre circle of daylight or, even better, a circle of mysterious blue light. I had no intention of depriving my 206 A of this feature, with the only stipulation that it would be possible to easily remove the additional lighting for trade fairs or exhibitions when the submarine is displayed on its stand. The solution in this case was to mount the diodes in the already existing openings on the upper deck. This involved mounting a LED at the front in the sonar bow combined with a reflective socket and another two in the conning tower. The LEDs project a blue light upwards, which looks great when the submarine is submerged. For a power supply it was necessary to drill a hole in the cover to take the pressure resistant plug. IP68 plugs worked well for this application.

The submarine's stern with cross rudders and low-noise, sickle-shaped propeller (photo: Detlef Franke).

The final modification for the moment, concerned, once more, the diving system. The diving tank was activated by a switch which causes the piston diving tank to either flood or deballast. A great degree of sensitivity is required to adjust the submarine so that it is almost still. You have to judge how long you need to run the pumps, bearing in mind that there is a time delay between running the motor and the reaction of the submarine. The new system now incorporates a bicycle speedometer. Combined with a magnet, this captures the gear-wheel revolutions in the pump and makes it possible to achieve a proportional adjustment over the total travel of the piston. The transmitter now has a throttle to regulate the pump rather than a switch.

Top Secret – the Narwal Project

In 1987 the Federal Navy issued a contract to develop the Narwal underwater transport device, class 740/03. The purpose of this device was to transport navy frogmen to where they were to operate in the coastal waters of the Baltic Sea.

Detailed view of the Narwal's bow. You can see the left and right mounted bow underwater headlights that are protected by metal brackets. A downwards pointing camera is located in the centre. The mine avoidance sonar is located behind the bow flap (photo: Detlef Franke).

The Narwal's transport frame. You can see the two containers on the right. These are transport containers for explosive devices that are attached to the end of the dive plane (photo: Detlef Franke).

The keel of the Narwal was laid in 1989. In October 1995 it obtained its Class Equivalence Certificate and was brought into service with the WTD 71 (Centre for Defence Technology).

In January 1996 the submarine required a major mechanical overhaul. When the cost of this work was established, the decision was taken to withdraw the submarine from service. The budget available for such work was small and at that time political tensions in Europe had abated. Today the submarine is on display in the Museum of Military History in Dresden.

The submarine was assigned to the Centre for Defence Technology (WTD) 71 in Eckernförde. It was put through its paces by the navy frogmen and divers of the WTD, who were trained in operating the device.

Since the Narwal never got past the trial stage, no official record was made of its existence. Indeed this is the first time it has featured in any literature. There is a logic behind its 'top secret' status in so much as it was an experimental military device and the need to keep the prying eyes at bay is understandable.

The hydrodynamic properties of the Narwal are excellent. It can be assumed that it had an impressive performance spectrum, although no exact data have ever been published.

Technical data	
Complement	a pilot, a co-pilot and three crew, who are deployed with the co-pilot in the target zone.
Water displacement	6 GRT (gross registered tonnes)
Mass	25,300 kg
Length	13,270 mm
Width	2,500 mm
Height	2,100 mm
Propulsion system	electric
Main propeller	15 KW (20.4 hp) – two vertical thrusters each developing 3 KW (4.1 hp).

A leap in underwater technology: the Class 212a

The four Type 212a submarines will give the German Navy the world's most modern non-nuclear submarines. They have been planned, designed and built by HDW Howaldswerke Deutsche Werft AG in Kiel in collaboration with TNSW Thyssen Nordseewerke in Emden. The Type 212a was based on the design for the 212. The project was revised in cooperation with the Italian Navy, which will likewise deploy these Type 212a submarines.

It differs fundamentally from other submarines with conventional propulsion systems in so far as it uses hybrid propulsion. This consists of a fuel cell system that does not require a supply of external air and a state of the art diesel-electric engine. The total propulsion system is encapsulated in a soundproof module, which is elastically supported in the submarine's structure. It drives a propeller that rotates slowly and extremely quietly. Consequently, the noise generated by its propeller and propulsion system is so little as to effectively minimise the chance of it being located.

In the case of conventional submarines the whole hull is manufactured from anti-magnetic steel. In the 212a it is only the pressure hull that is built from this material, while the external body of the hull is made of plastic. Flaps cover all the openings on the outside of the vessel. This eliminates any water turbulence that might generate noise. The dive planes and the x-shaped stern rudder have been similarly optimised for streamlined performance. As a result of all these features the Type 212a hardly makes a sound when travelling underwater.

The submarine is equipped with a complex sensor system. The sonar suite consists of a main cylindrical array which is concealed in the bow and which locates by means of hydrophone. This is supplemented by two flank array antennas, mounted on the outside of the submarine, and one towed array antenna that monitors the dead acoustic space behind the screw of the vessel itself. For target location there are three bases on each side to detect high frequency active impulses – such as the 'ping' of torpedoes. Finally, an intercept sonar is mounted on the conning tower. An active mine-avoidance sonar serves to locate and avoid anchored submarine mines. Separate sensors measure the submarine's own acoustic signature.

The sensor technology also includes two further elements: two periscopes (an attack and observation periscope) which protrude from the pressure hull. Both are fitted with distance measuring devices. The observation periscope also has a heat-imaging device. The attack periscope also carries the ESM aerials (electronic support measure – to

The first time the submarine entered the water (copyright HDW Peter Neumann).

Cutaway section of the Type 212, which clearly shows how the space is used (copyright HDW).

Technical data	
Length	approx. 56 m
Pressure hull diameter	approx. 7 m
Displacement	1,450 t
Complement	27 crew
Propulsion	diesel-electric/fuel cell system

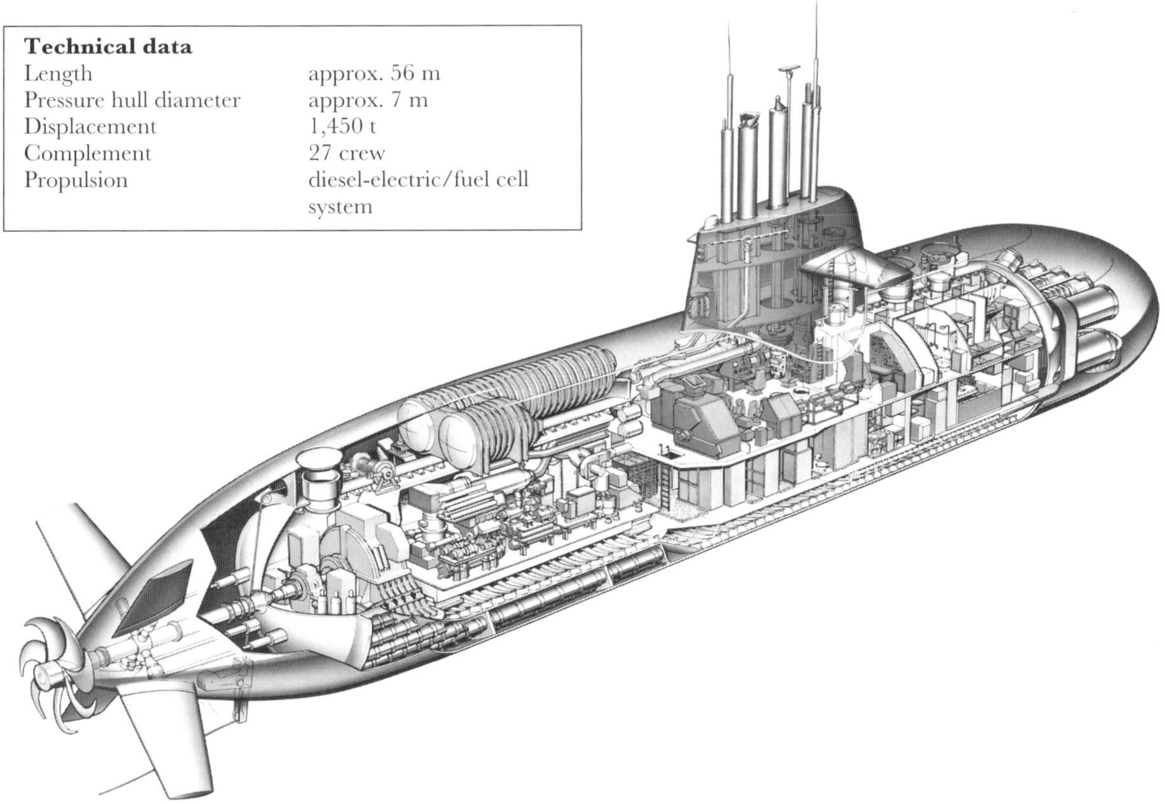

The christening of the U 31 on March 20th 2003 at the Howaldtswerken Deutsche Werft AG in Kiel (copyright HDW Peter Neumann).

detect radar, for example) and the GPS (global positioning system) aerial. Other extendable equipment includes radar and snorkel masts, as well as two long-distance rod antennas.

The submarine is armed with heavyweight torpedoes of the 'Seehecht' type. These have high performance propulsion and this enables them to reach targets over large distances and thus exploit the submarine's full location range. Likewise there are systems to defend against a torpedo attack.

All significant information is collected and managed by a basic guidance and weapon delivery system. The propulsion and operations technology is likewise controlled automatically through the integrated steering and control centre.

The submarine has a crew of 25. They are trained to deal with the large operational range and extended stay in the operations zone. As is usual on all other submarines in the Federal Navy the crew operates in a three-watch system. The separation of the living quarters from the operations and business area means that the accommodation is comfortable by comparison.

On the other hand, the technical and guidance command centres (control room and central operations room) are joined into one.

Off on its first sea trials in the Baltic Sea (copyright Stefan Lipsky).

Drawing: Carl Schröder

U31 surfaced in the pool.

Type 212a to a scale of 1:32

Submarine meets provide an excellent opportunity to show model making colleagues what you have built or intend to build. So it was in the summer of 2000 in Aurich on the Ihlow Sea, when, at the invitation of the Aurich Model Ship Association, a large number of model makers from the international submarine association SONAR got together.

SONAR member Carl Schröder from Bremerhaven was also there and presented his new construction project. He opened the boot of his car and pulled out a massive plastic tube with the words, "This will be the middle section of my new 212". He had planned to build the model to a scale of 1:32. This equates to a length of 1.73 m. The tube is 21.9 cm in diameter and everyone there was left in no doubt that it was going to be a particularly big submarine. Such demanding models are certainly not built in a day. It is almost impossible to find any standard parts and so it took him two and half years from start to launch to complete this impressive

The middle section of the finished submarine with the upper deck removed. The equipment frame for the pneumatically powered extendable equipment is screwed into the rectangular-shaped recess. The main diving tank with a volume of 4.8 litres is located underneath.

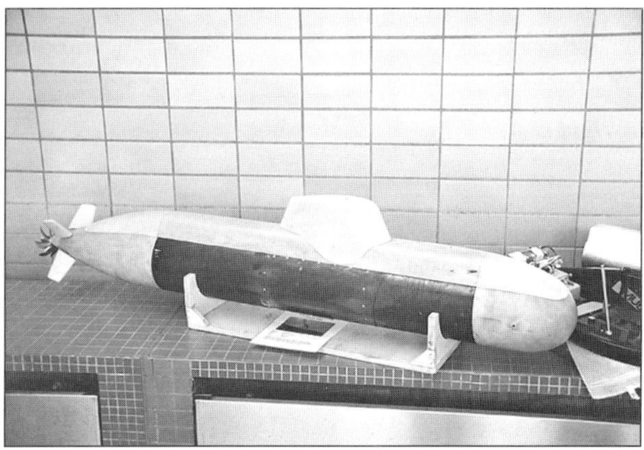

The U31 still as a shell on a SONAR event, held together with the submarine fleet in Eckernförde. Here you can still see clearly the middle section consisting of a plastic tube, as described in the text.

A close up view of the stern with the rudder system and the propeller. The X-rudder configuration gives a high level of mobility. The rudder system's servos and the drive motor are permanently fixed into the stern section.

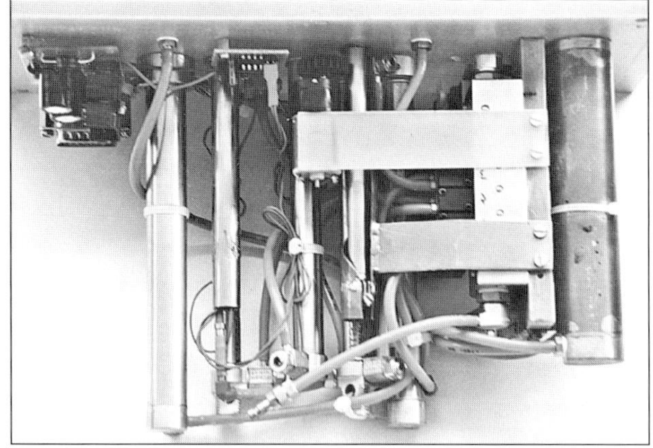

The lower section of the extendable equipment. You can clearly see the pressure cylinder and the hose system.

model. Indeed it turned out to be so impressive that Carl Schröder was invited to show his submarine to the constructors of the original, HDW, in Kiel.

The model of the German Navy's U31 submarine is equipped with two diving systems. The main system is a compressed air tank that is used to pump air into the main diving tank in the middle section of the submarine. In addition, another two piston-tanks are incorporated, one in the bow and one in the stern. They can be used for trimming, either individually or proportionally. Should you want to lay the submarine 'on the bottom' for example, these tanks can also be used to provide downward force.

Additionally, the compressed air is used to operate the six extendable devices. One of these is the snorkel that has the function of ventilating the submarine when the compressors are running.

The bow contains the compressed air tank and the bow jet pumps. Next come the batteries and the front piston-tank, after which are electronic components as, for example, the piston-tank controller. The sequence continues with the compressors and valves for air-input and to flood the tanks. The main tank is located in the middle with a box at the centre to take the extendable equipment. The section after this has more batteries and electronic components such as piston-tank controller, drive controller etc. Then come the last set of batteries and the rear piston-tank. Finally, the motor and the servos for the rudder are located in the stern section.

The submarine is dynamically stabilised in a longitudinal direction by an electronic pitch and depth controller and maintained at the depth that has been set on the transmitter.

The bow and hull section which are inserted into the middle section. In spite of a total length of 1.73 m no centimetre of space is wasted. The number of components incorporated also explains the weight of 51.5 kg. Two 0.5 litre trim tanks can be clearly seen at the top of the sections.

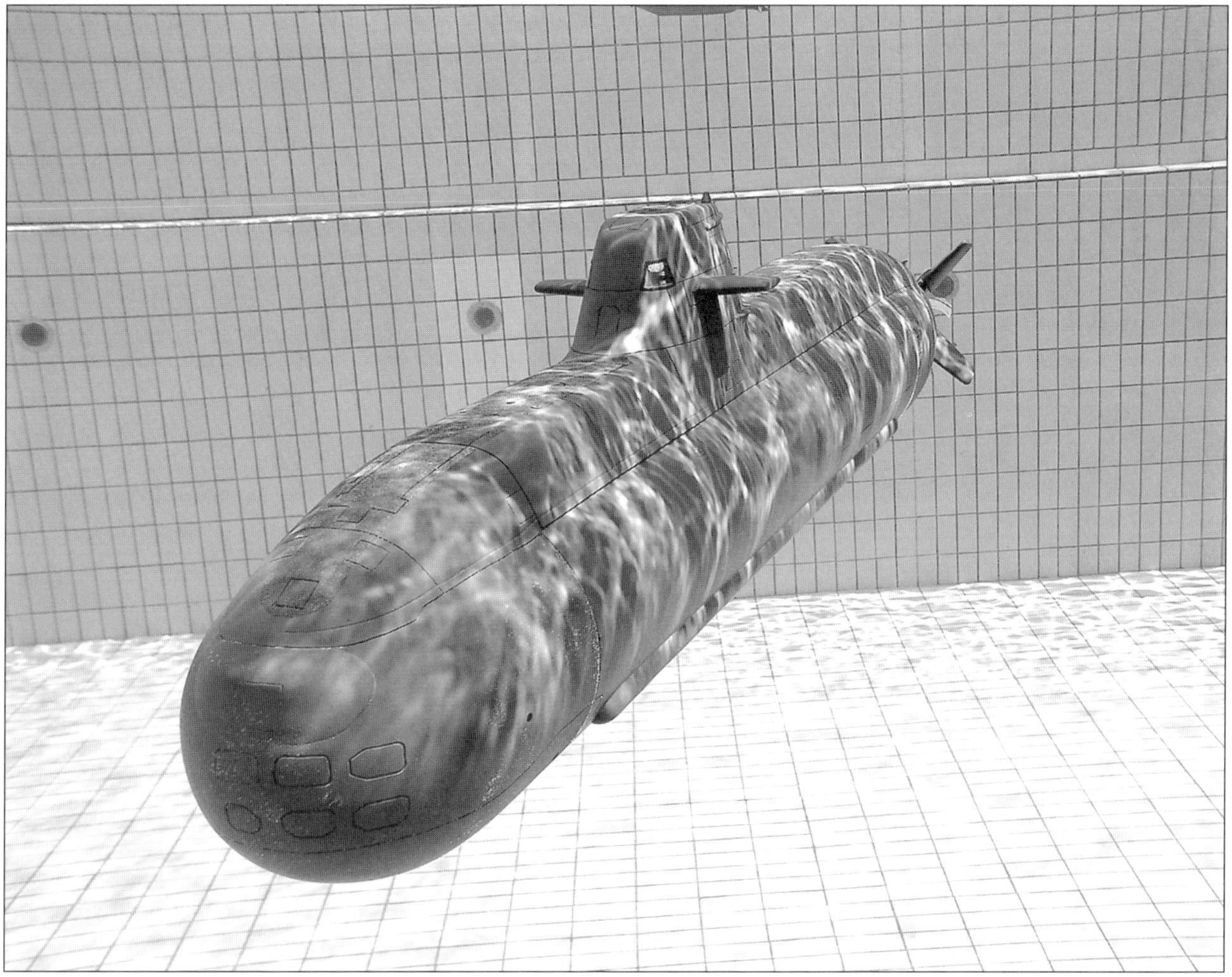

The U31 in its element. For the submarine to perform to its full potential a very large pool is really required.

Technical data

Length	1.73 m
Diameter	219 mm
Weight	surfaced 51.5 kg/ submerged 56.8 kg
Main diving tank	2 x 0.5 litres
Battery capacity	43.5 amps
Compressed air tank	21 litres at 6 bar
Diving depth	max. 10 m
Speed	approx 10 km/h
Construction time	2 1/2 years
Functions	Drive speed controller Dive planes, nominal depth Rudder Depth controller Filling the diving-tanks with air Bow piston-tank Stern piston-tank Bow jet rudder left/right Individual activation of all extendable equipment Emergency system, surfacing if transmitter fails.

The upper section with the six extendable devices. Air is sucked in through the submarine's snorkel by a compressor to operate the diving system and the extendable equipment, just like the original.

Chapter 7

Atomic Submarines

The giant of the deep: Russia's Typhoon Class

Technical data	
Length	172.80 m
Width	23.30 m
Draught	11.50 m
Propulsion	two pressure-water reactors, Geared steam turbines each developing 190 MW Connected to two shafts for a maximum speed of 26 knots submerged.
Water displacement	surfaced 18,500 t submerged 26,500 t
Dive depth	max. 400 m
Complement	149 crew
Maximum period at sea	120 days
Completion of the first unit	1981, the latest submarine so far came into service in 1989.
Armament	20 SS-N 20 missiles in a large compartment in front of the conning tower. 6 calibre 533 mm bow torpedo tubes, with 22 torpedoes available.

The original

The submarines of the Typhoon Class are the biggest that have ever been built. Indeed, it makes sense to talk about underwater ships. The inside of this submarine type consists of two parallel cylinders, each approx. 130 metres in length and containing their own reactor and propulsion train. This explains why the ship is unusually wide.

A third, shorter cylinder with a diameter of approx. 6 metres is located directly beneath the conning tower and contains the control centre. The way the submarine is constructed from several cylinders is somewhat unusual, yet it does go back to the first J.P. Holland designs and has already been used in the Dutch Tonjin Class.

You will not find this giant in western waters. As a floating nuclear weapon base its sphere of operations is the North Polar Sea.

Typhoon to a scale of 1:100

The original is the biggest submarine in the world and the model is also constructed to impressive proportions. SONAR member, Michael Weidner built the submarine from a GRP hull as supplied by Kehrer.

To a scale of 1:100 the Typhoon is 1.70 m long, 22.5 cm wide and the hull is 16.5 cm high or 28 cm with the conning tower.

You would expect a submarine with such a large hull volume to likewise break all weight records. Yet, it actually only weighs 18.5 kg, which is due to the fact that inside the outer hull there is a pressure hull made of Makrolon. This is 90 cm long, has a diameter of 12 cm and contains all the equipment required for diving and the operation of the submarine. The diving system comprises two proportionally controlled Engel tanks. Each has a volume of 500 ml and is converted to operate at 12 volts. The system is supported by a pitch/depth controller.

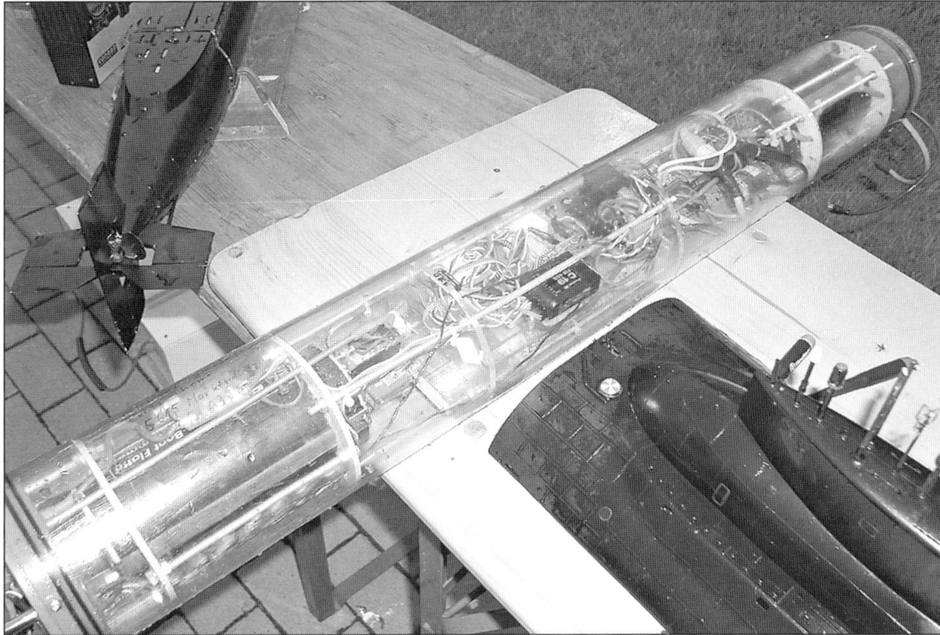

The main Makrolon pressure hull has been detached to show the equipment frame.

The two 12 volt Bühler propulsion motors as well as the servos for the rear dive planes and rudder are located in their own pressure-hull, which is likewise made of Makrolon. They sit in the stern and are connected to the main pressure hull by a waterproof plug and socket system. The Typhoon is equipped with a bow jet rudder for better manoeuvrability.

The propulsion motors and the diving tanks are powered by 10 cells (=12 V/6,000 mAh), while five cells supply power to the receiver (=6 V/2,400 mAh).

As in the original, the dive planes are designed to be retractable; they are controlled by waterproof servos.

Once the submarine is submerged and trimmed it looks really imposing underwater. Due to its length it is obviously not very manoeuvrable and it needs to be driven with some circumspection. However, by its very nature this submarine does not belong in small pools and lakes.

Chapter 8

Mastery Of The Deep

At the seas' deepest point: the Bathyskaphe in Trieste

Original

In the 1930s and 40s, the Swiss physicist and designer, Auguste Picard, made his reputation researching the earth's atmosphere and cosmic rays at high altitudes. He ascended to a height of 55,000 feet into the stratosphere in a pressure tight capsule attached to a gas-filled balloon.

With his son, Jacques, a sea biologist, he then re-formulated the principle of being 'lighter than air' to explore the sea depths. He constructed the 'Bathyskaphe' (Greek for 'ship of the deep').

The diving vehicle was ballasted by petrol filled tanks (since petrol is lighter than water) and was pulled down into the deep by cast-iron pellets. The pellets were held in place by a strong electro-magnet. Once the required depth was reached, sufficient pellets were jettisoned in order to hold the vessel at this depth or to allow it to rise again.

The precursors to this were the constructions called 'FRNS II and 'Archimedes'. They were the first to make possible a step-by-step exploration of the sea depths. In August 1954 the 'Archimedes', which is now owned by the French government, dived to a depth of 4,048 metres, marking a new milestone in deep-sea exploration.

In 1953, supported by the citizens of Trieste, who contributed in large measure to the project's financing, the Picards built a larger 'Bathyskaphe' and christened it 'Trieste'.

The 'Trieste' displaced 50.8 t when empty and 152.4 t when filled with petrol. The upper tank was 18.10 metres long and 3.50 m wide. It had a theoretical capacity of 106 tons of petrol. The pellet ballast was secured magnetically in two silo-shaped containers located in the upper tank and weighed 9.00 t or 16 t after the refit. Two inflatable buoyancy tanks were located at the ends of the tank. These raised the waterline when the vessel was surfaced. The pressure capsule was made of a special steel alloy; it was attached underneath the tank and connected by a 90 cm wide tunnel. The walls of the capsule were 8.89 cm thick, with additional strengthening around the windows. Picard used conically shaped Plexiglas for the windows.

The internal diameter of the capsule was 2.16 m and provided space for a crew of two. There was not much room at all to move, since this capsule also contained all the technical equipment such as echo sounder and underwater telephone, as well as all the breathing equipment with their CO^2 absorbers and the two bottles of compressed air. The external lighting consisted of two quicksilver vapour lamps and spotlights with light bulbs. When fitted out, the capsule enabled the submarine to dive to 3,048 m.

The submarine's livery really in no way encapsulated the modern spirit of the 1960s, since its main purpose was safety. The black and white stripes on the shell of the tank mark the welding seams. These were emphasised in colour to facilitate a more effective control (photo: Erich Frotzler).

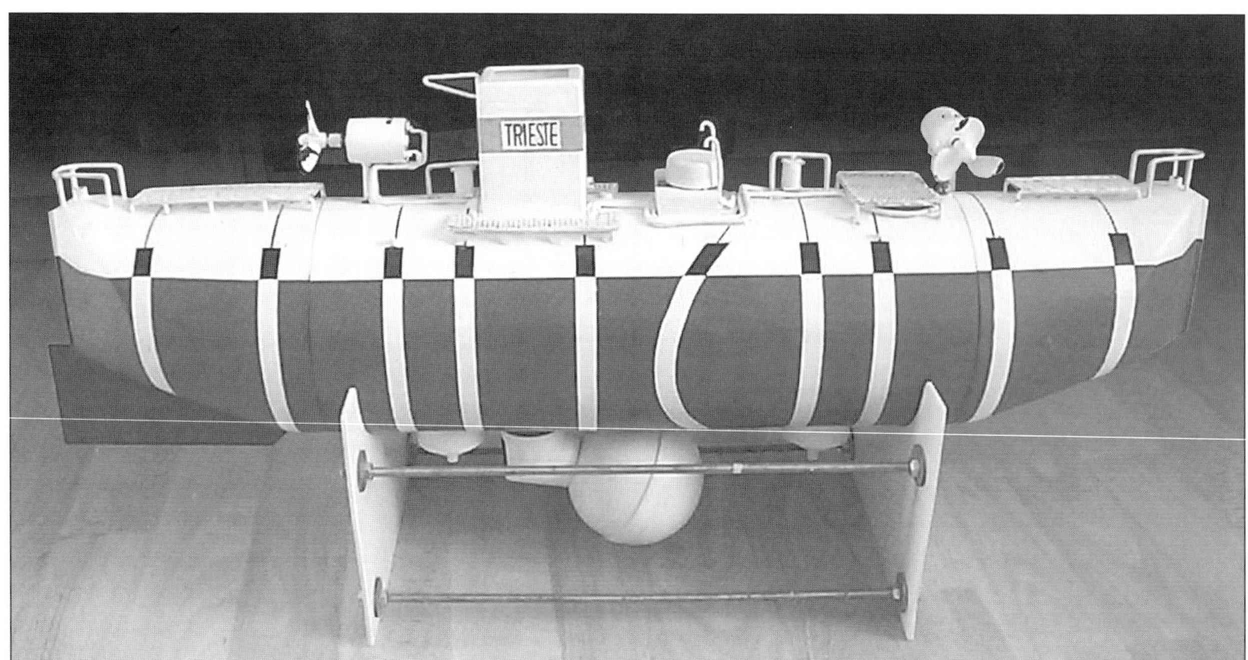

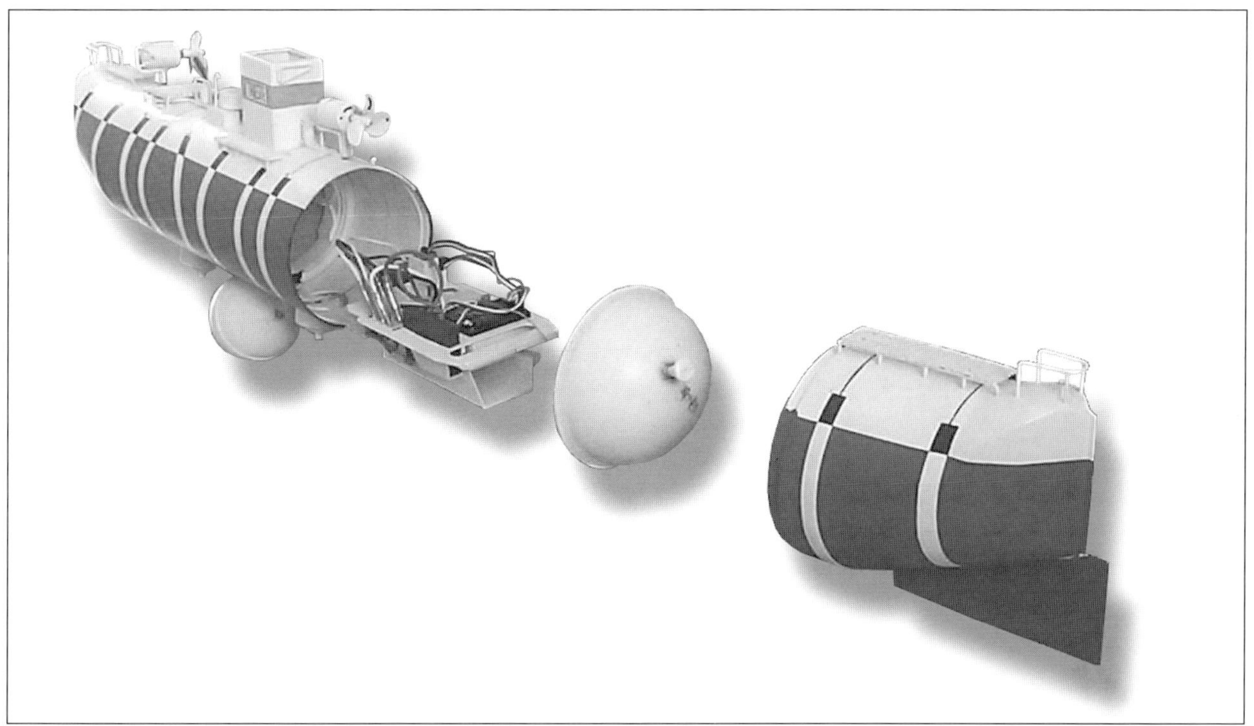

The 'Trieste' taken apart with the equipment plate pulled out, the front seal and bow section (photo: Erich Frotzler).

In 1957 the US Office of Naval Research purchased the 'Trieste' and fitted it out for greater depths. Krupp AG manufactured a new pressure capsule. It had a weight of 13 tonnes and a wall thickness of 12.7 cm. The strengthening around the windows was now extended to 17.78 cm and the capacity of the tanks was likewise increased.

In 1959 a depth of 5,642 metres was reached and on January 23rd 1960 Navy Lieutenant Don Walsh and Jacques Picard came to rest on the bottom of the Mariana Trough at a depth of 10,740 metres. The deepest point on the globe had been reached.

Life still exists at that depth, but since then no one has ever gone back to see.

In the mid 1990s the Mariana Trough was again explored, this time by a Japanese research institute using high-tech ROVs (remote operated vehicles). In spite of the fact that technology has developed in quantum leaps, this expedition also encountered major difficulties.

In its service life the 'Trieste' completed 128 dives and made a decisive contribution to deep-sea exploration. It also played a significant role for the US Navy in the search for the 'Thresher', the atomic submarine that sank in 1963.

These operations also clearly revealed a major weakness in the Bathyskaphe. Dr. Robert D. Ballard in his book 'The Deep – Great Expeditions into the World of Eternal Darkness' hit the nail on the head when he wrote, that it resembled more a lift than a submarine. Its 2 hp oil-filled electric motors helped it achieve a speed of only one knot. This made it almost impossible to carry out a horizontal analysis of the seabed.

The time was ripe for mobile, deep-sea research submarines. More about this in the chapter about the 'Alvin'.

The 'Trieste I' to a scale of 1:25

In the course of constructing his 'Bathyskaphe' August Picard introduced new concepts for submarine design. This may be due to the fact that a 'Bathyskapthe' is more like a 'diving hot-air balloon' than a submarine.

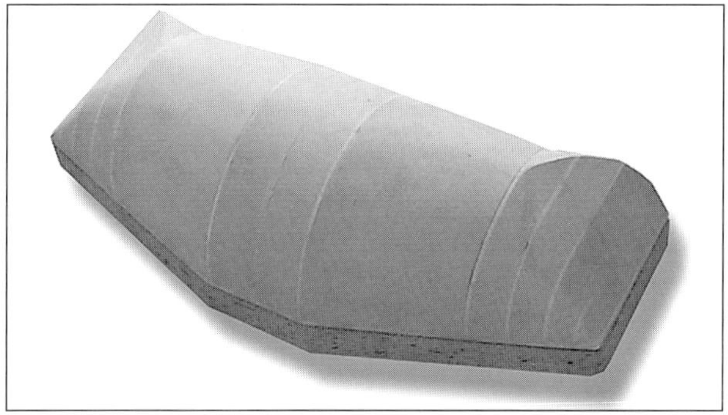

The master profile for the vac-formed bow and stern sections (photo: Erich Frotzler).

However, for Erich Frotzler from Vienna, it provided all the encouragement he needed to build his model 'Trieste', incorporating ideas that were likewise unusual for model submarine makers.

His 'Trieste I' is built to a scale of 1:25, has a total length of 67.7 cm, a width of 13.8 cm and a height from the capsule to the tower of 29.5 cm.

The model's pressure hull consists of a 12 cm long acrylic tube with a diameter of 12.8 cm and a wall thickness of 5.0 mm. Two layers of polystyrene panels are wrapped around and adhered to the acrylic tube to achieve the scale length and thickness, up until the point where the slope of the submarine's bow or stern begins. The bow and the stern are exactly the same shape. Both sections are likewise made of polystyrene which is vac-formed over a mould. To seal the internally located pressure hull, Erich Frotzler built two semicircular locking sections, which as one might imagine, were also vac-formed.

On its way into the deep (photo Erich Frotzler).

The remote control components: receiver, three robbe Rohkraft 100 speed controllers and the 7.2 V/1,800 mA drive battery are all mounted on the equipment plate, which in turn sits in the pressure hull. It is designed so that the technical plate can be removed from the pressure hull.

In contrast to other designs the 'Trieste' does not have a diving tank. Yet, at the same time the model does not dive dynamically (through forward motion).

The dive propulsion clears up this little mystery. Hidden in the rear section of the model's hull, where in the original the inlet for the front pellet silo was located, there is a vertically directed electric motor. It is incorporated in a duct and its propeller propulsion counteracts any remaining tendency for the submarine to rise, thus causing it to sink.

Another unusual feature of this design is the way that this motor, like the two drive motors, can be driven free-flooded in water. This appears to have no adverse effect on the Speed 280 type motors and, after many years of use, the model is still powered by the original motors.

The propulsion motors mounted on the deck are rigidly fixed and cannot be rotated. The rear motor is set at right angles to the direction of travel and functions as a rudder. The front motor provides forward propulsion. These two 280 motors give the model a speed that is considerably higher than that of the original.

On the original, the tower is no more than a wave breaker protecting the entry tunnel. The tower on the model functions to hide the connection between the bow and the stern section and is designed to be detachable, so as to provide better access for maintenance.

The original's pressure capsule underneath the hull is used in the model as a 'ballast keel'. It was made using a half-globe of plaster, such as can be obtained at any model makers, that serves as a vac-forming mould and is processed in the standard way.

Erich Frotzler also came up with a special solution to the ON/OFF switch. When he built his model, no one had heard of the magnetic switches we use today and he took the bottle lock from a PET bottle together with the cap. When the cap is unscrewed, it opens up the space to switch on the normal receiver switch by hand. You have to look twice to see that this component is a lock. After all, the 'Trieste' was a research submarine and, depending on the assignment, it often had different attachments fixed to its hull.

Chapter 9

Underwater Holiday Adventure

The 'Jaqueline' SM 100/50 Tourist Submarine

The original

Since the time that submarines were first used for scientific sea exploration, the opportunity to so discover flora and fauna has been restricted to only a few researchers. For those who unfortunately do not happen to be researchers and who are nevertheless interested in seeing with their own eyes the fascinating deep-sea world, the only other possibility has been to undertake training to acquire diving skills. In this case, however, depth is the limiting factor. 40 m is the safe maximum depth for anyone who dives for fun and not everyone enjoys jumping into cold water.

This gap in the market has been filled by tourist submarines, which make it possible for everyone to book a trip underwater and to experience this fascination.

The 'Jacqueline' type SM 100/50 has been developed by the Finnish companies, Wärtsila Aktiebolag and Global Submarines Oy Ltd. The submarine was built in Belgium and is based in Eilat/Israel.

The 'Jacqueline' is 22.20 metres long, 3,03 metres wide, 6.80 metres high and weighs 93.1 tonnes.

The operating depth is 100 m. The maximum load is 5 tonnes which equates to 48 passengers and two crew members.

In contrast to submarines designed for military use, there is no possibility of charging the batteries of the electro-

The SM 100/50 on diving trials near Malta (copyright Global Submarines Oy Ltd.).

The original in Eilat/Israel (photo Horst Kiner).

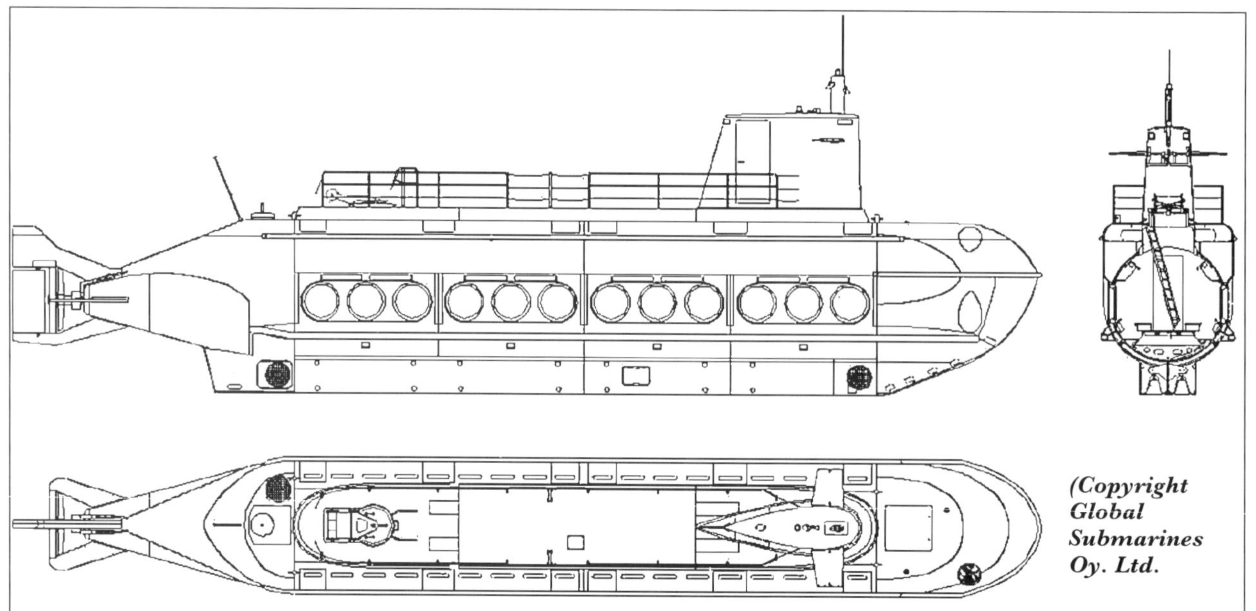
(Copyright Global Submarines Oy. Ltd.

View of the main pressure hull (copyright Global Submarines Oy. Ltd.).

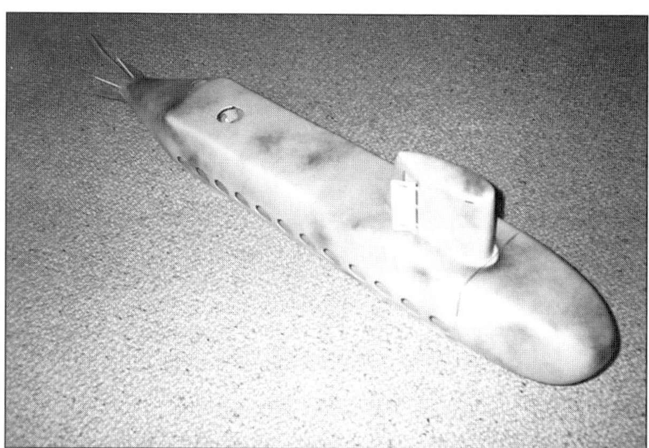
Basic hull construction (photo: Horst Kiner).

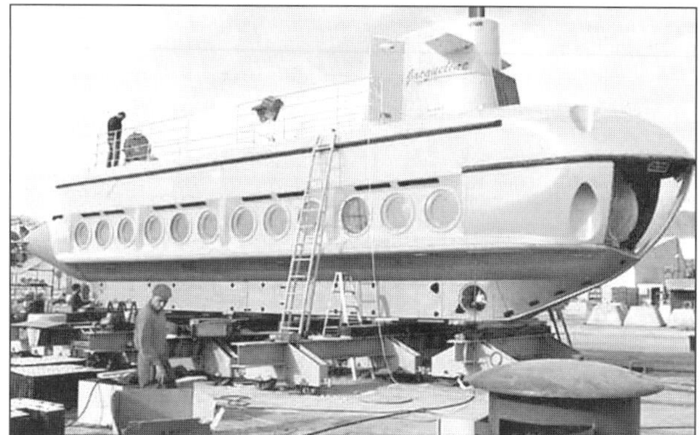

The submarine is almost complete and lies in dry dock in the shipyard (copyright Global Submarines Oy. Ltd.).

hydraulic propulsion when travelling on the surface. This can only be done from land.

The main propulsion develops 80 KW, driving a motor and a shaft, while the addition of four 10 KW manoeuvre thrusters provides a high level of mobility.

For operational safety the submarines of this class are constructed with a high power upward thrust. The ballast system is constructed to take on a possible 10 t of water. To evacuate the tanks it has a compressed air capacity of 2,000 litres. A quick release weight of 2,000 kg in the keel adds a further element of operational safety.

600 litres of oxygen pressurised to 200 bar supply the air required for breathing.

Combined with the existing dual breathing air preparation system, this gives a supply of 12 hours + 72 hours emergency supply.

Each trip lasts 45 minutes and an escort submarine is in attendance for the full duration both to ensure the necessary safety and also to let out a diver who has food to attract fish for the submarine guests. Conditions on the submarine are comfortable; every two guests share a large porthole and they all enjoy an air-conditioned deep-sea dive.

The 'Jacqueline' to a scale of 1:16

At a model submarine meeting in Nuremberg SONAR member Horst Kiner from Ratzenried spotted an advertisement for an event. It featured the 'Jacqueline'. With the support of Rudi Schwarzmeier more documentation was quickly organised to begin the construction.

The submarine is built to a scale of 1:16. This makes it 1.40 m long. The external pressure tight jacket is made from

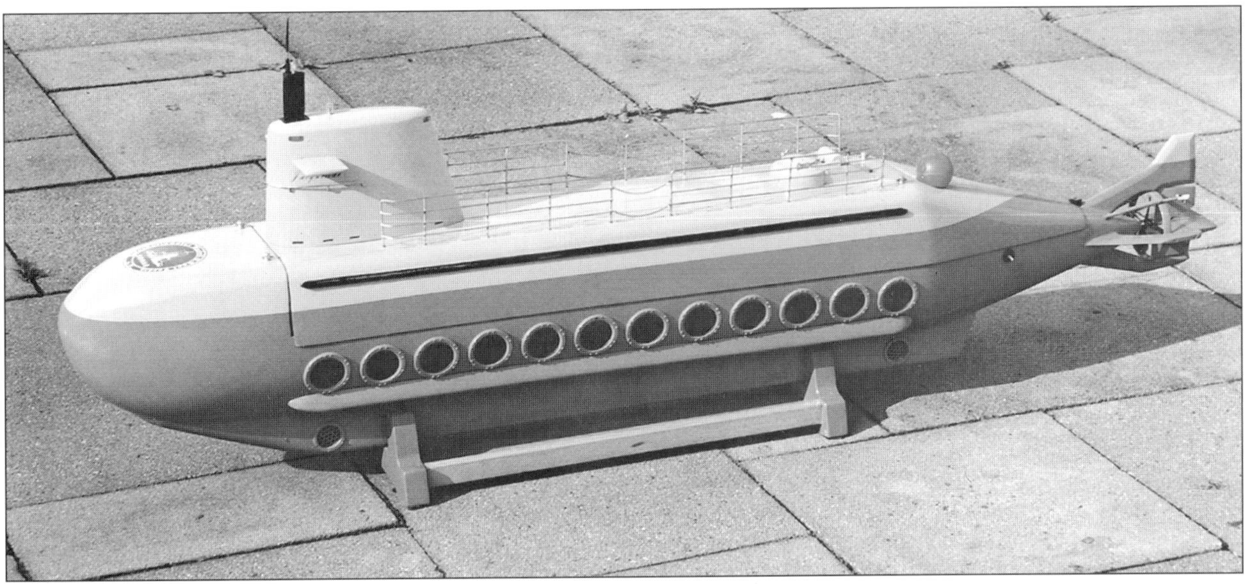

The individual sections of the hull; on the left of the picture you can see a part of the pressure hull.

GRP. All the technical equipment is located inside a Plexiglas tube with the dimensions: 160 x 630 mm.

The only components to penetrate to the outside are the propeller's drive shaft and the rods for the rear dive planes. In contrast to the original, it is this plane that is used for the diving and not the one on the tower.

The diving system consists of a piston tank with a volume of one litre; however this does not raise the submarine to the desired keel waterline.

At the time of writing this book Horst Kiner was in the middle of converting the submarine to a compressed air control system. We look forward to the next meeting in Nuremberg.

Right: The 'Jacqueline' submerges in the outdoor pool in Kaiserslautern. The turquoise coloured water detracts greatly from the blue/yellow livery. On top of the stern you can see the submarine's emergency buoy.

Chapter 10

Research, Rescue and Work Submarines

The 'Delta' Research Submarine. At home on any sea

The original

The 'Delta' is a two-man research submarine, which is designed and operated by Delta Oceanographics. It was built in 1983 and since then has completed more than 5,900 dives. The most publicised was the discovery of the 'Lusitania' off the coast of Ireland by Prof. Robert Ballard.

The 'Delta' is a small submarine. It is 4.60 m long, 1.10 m wide, 1.80 m high and weighs 2.2 t. Due to its size, the submarine operates globally. It was no surprise, therefore, that the author tracked down his contact in the company, Rich Slater, not at home in California, but rather in Italy. What was the 'Delta' researching in Italy? Rich Slater would not say.

The submarine is propelled by an electric motor, which is powered by eight 6 volt batteries. In spite of the small dimensions and a maximum load of 250 kg, inclusive of the crew members, the submarine contains a wealth of high-tech equipment. Indeed, a 12, 24 and 48 volt supply enables all necessary on board devices to be operated.

For visual research the submarine is equipped with a high resolution Kodak DC 260 digital camera on the tower. A Sony DCR TRV 900 3CCD digital video camera can also be fitted as an alternative. There is also a CD-writer on board to record what is seen. In fact it is not just responsible for the processing of visual images, since it also uses a special computer programme to log each dive.

There are two compasses for underwater navigation, a fluxgate and a magnetic compass. These are complemented by a GPS system and a high-resolution digital sonar device. High intensity lamps provide illumination for video work or for manipulation. Depending what technical equipment the submarine is carrying, these can be 250 to 400 watts. As is the case for almost all other well-known research submarines, the equipment is modular. Each deployment demands its own special equipment, carried either on board the submarine or attached to the outside.

The 'Delta' has a unique appearance. In spite of its small

Side view of the 'Delta' (copyright Delta Oceanographics).

The 'Delta' at its launch in 1983. You can clearly see the glazing of the front diving tank (copyright Delta Oceanographics).

View from the front starboard side. The dive plane is not attached (copyright Delta Oceanographics).

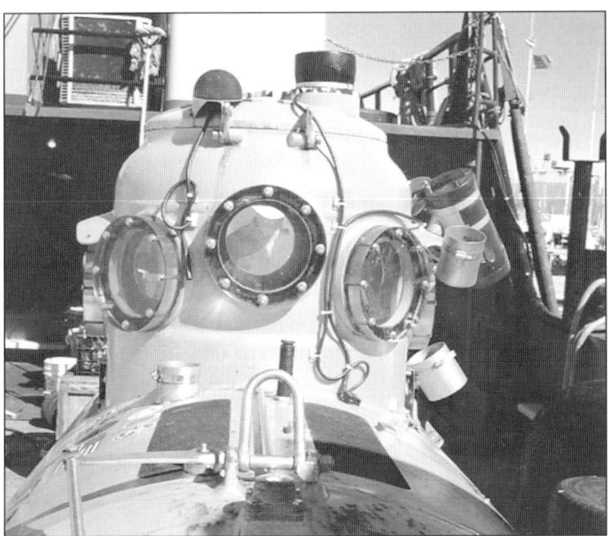

The tower viewed from the rear. In front there is a lifting lug used for crane transport (copyright Delta Oceanographics).

Detailed view of the tower and the attached searchlights (copyright Delta Oceanographics).

size, it has 19 observation portholes. Even the dive plane in its unorthodox position in front of the tower is made of Plexiglas. The researchers should not miss a thing.

Safety on this submarine is also paramount. During the expedition to find the 'Lusitania' the 'Delta' got trapped in the remains of the wreck. However, it completed a straight-forward ascent to the surface by simply releasing the stern module. This is separated from the passenger cabin by a bulkhead. Indeed, the survival systems on board are designed to operate for 144 man-hours.

The 'Delta' has a maximum dive depth of 520 metres. Its operational dive depth is stated as 365 metres. No research submarine is ever very quick. It cruises at a speed of 1.5 knots and the maximum possible speed is 3.5 knots.

The port side view of the stern. Attached to the cone is one of the rear-mounted searchlights (copyright Delta Oceanographics).

Detailed view of the starboard portholes (copyright Delta Oceanographics).

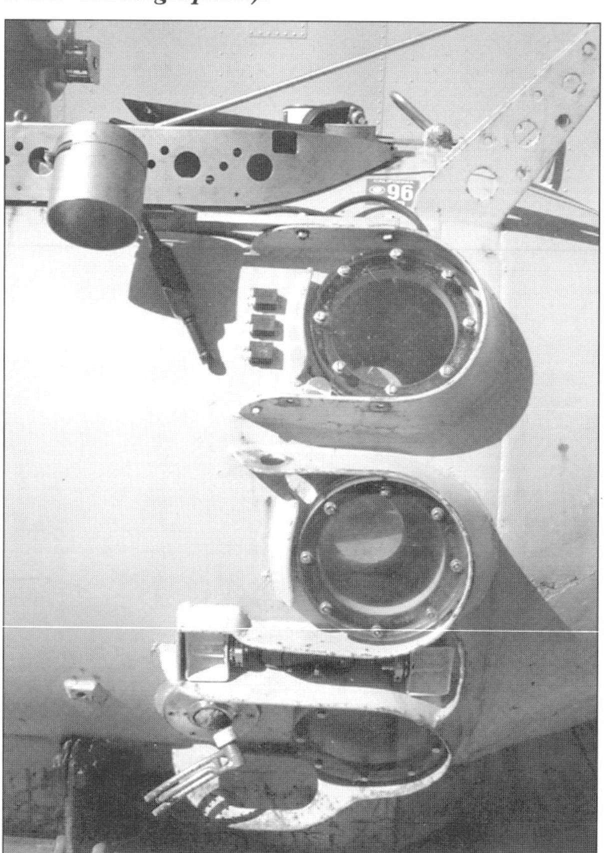

The model of the 'Delta'

The model of the 'Delta' is built to a scale of 1:8. The construction kit can be obtained from 'Norbert Brüggen Modell-U-Boot-Spezialitäten'. Submarine model-makers associate Norbert Brüggen with particularly high-quality model submarine kits. This submarine is no exception and represents a really positive extension to the range of mostly military submarines.

The model consists principally of parts cast in polyurethane (also called resin). The Plexiglas panels and many polystyrene and aluminium add-on components are supplied as CNC-milled parts.

The tubular hull is designed to withstand pressure to a destruction dive depth of 9.5 m. Most submarine model makers would freely admit that they would never want to take their model to such a depth. Nevertheless, it is good to know that it does have a certain integral security.

The submarine is steered by dive planes and a rudder as well as a speed controller. The dive technology is a system recently developed by Norbert Brüggen. It uses neither a piston diving tank nor a system based on compressed air. Instead, a sealed hose pump regulates the depth by flooding or emptying a sack made of PE-film.

This system also makes it possible to incorporate tanks in submarines, which would previously have been too small for such systems.

The scale of 1:8 also enables features of the original to be copied in detail. If you placed a pilot figure next to the submarine, it would have to be 28 cm high.

Models of research submarines have one overriding feature: their functionality. If you have ever sailed your submarine at night in a pool or a clear water lake and have switched on the searchlights, you will certainly be able to share this fascination. Ultra-bright light diodes are recom-

The model is beautifully detailed. The stern section has been pulled out slightly, while the dive plane is still to be assembled.

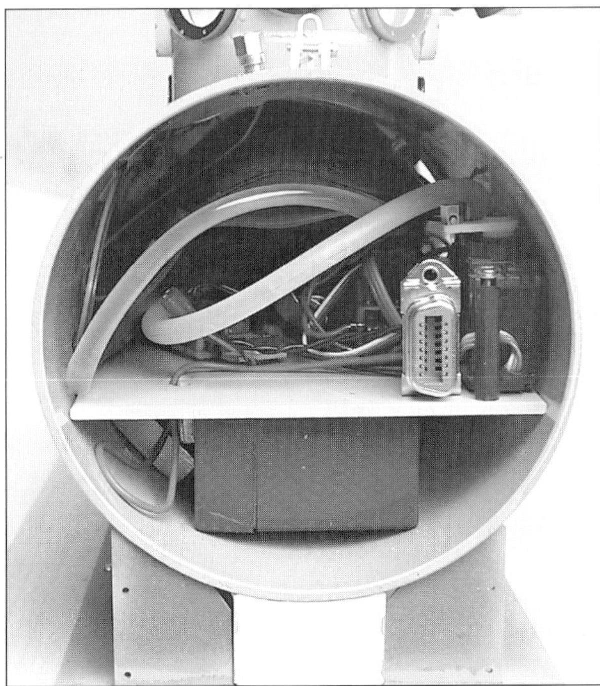

View of the inside of the hull. You can see the panel that carries the technical equipment and the lead-gel battery underneath. The hose-lines are part of the diving system, while the electrical connections to the stern are bundled in a Centronics plug (copyright Norbert Brüggen).

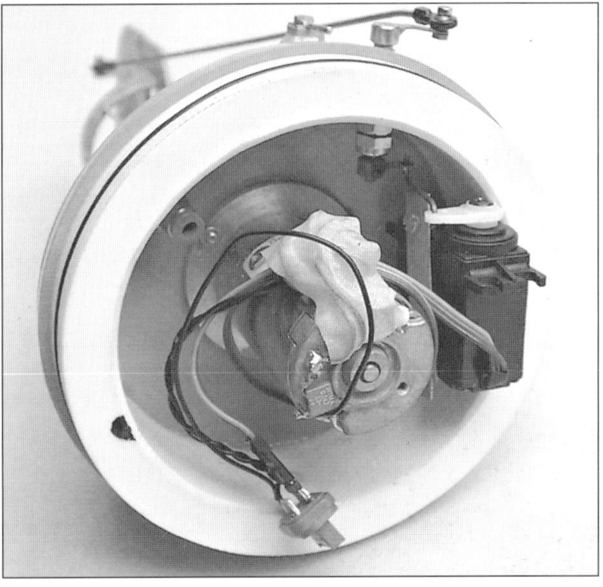

The stern of the 'Delta' with the moulded ring lock. The motor is mounted in the middle, while on the right is the servo for the rudder and on the left the connection nipple for the diving tank (copyright Norbert Brüggen).

mended for this application; such a set of lights is available for the 'Delta'.

Another highlight involves bringing live underwater pictures to the surface via a video camera. An easy alternative is to install a CMOS colour camera in the submarine and to send the data via a coaxial cable to a suitable television monitor. The expensive alternative involves the transmission of picture and sound data using a radio link. Extremely compact transmitters and receivers are used for this application. Moreover, you need to take into consideration that water does not conduct radio waves and you will need to locate the transmitter in a little buoy on the surface of the water.

The 'Delta' sailing with a camera on board. The transmitter buoy for video transmission can be seen at the top of the picture.

A multi-functional tower hatch. It was not anticipated in the original design and represents a challenge in terms of the model-making technology. A video camera is mounted in the tower.

A swarm of five 'Deltas' shows the popularity of this extraordinary model.

Driving a model submarine using only a camera image is a real challenge. In natural waters you tend to quickly lose visual contact with the submarine and it is only the transmitter buoy that gives some indication of where the submarine might be.

Depending on the dive depth and the length of the coaxial cable to the transmitter buoy, the pilot is left in the dark as to the direction in which the submarine is steering and how deep it is. Help comes from professional diving equipment. A small diving compass and a depth gauge, which both appear in the bottom corner of the camera viewer, provide the pilot with the necessary information. These instruments can be removed if they are not required.

Bruker 'Seahorse II' – Hightech 'Made in Germany'

The Original

In 1983 the Karlsruhe based Bruker Meerestechnik GmbH built the 'Seahorse II'. In the preceding 10 years the company has successfully constructed work submarines of the type 'Mermaid'. However, the Seahorse concept was a real breakthrough for research or offshore applications.

In contrast to the other work submarines, the 'Seahorse II' is designed as an autonomous submarine. The Bruker engineers, led by engineering graduate, Jörg Haas, realised that the use of submarines such as the 'Mermaid' in a commercial environment involved a very high cost of supplying the submarine.

Up until that point all the submarines available on the market had to be brought to the place of deployment by a mother ship and could only operate within a small radius of this ship.

Systems that rely on a mother ship are essentially weather-dependent. If the wind strength or wave height exceeds a certain limit, the submarines cannot be deployed. For deployment in the North Sea this results in a time window of only approx. 100 days per year, when the systems can be used.

A work submarine of the type 'Mermaid V', the precursor to the 'Seahorse'. These submarines were similarly designed for a rugged, offshore environment. Equipped with an additional pressure-resistant compartment for the divers as well as a dive-lock, it could work on seabed installations according to the saturation dive procedure. This submarine type had a special feature: the extendable support legs. These ensure that the gap between the submarine and the seabed is sufficient to enable the diver to get out of the submarine. Two manipulators support the diver's work. Such was the success of this design concept that the Yugoslavian Navy had two submarines of this type built as rescue submarines.

The 'Seahorse' on the way to a trial. In the tower is graduate engineer, Jörg Haas (photo: Jörg Haas/ BMT archive).

Aft view of the submarine; you can clearly see the raised snorkel mast (photo: Jörg Haas/BMT archive).

The 'Seahorse' is defined as an autonomous submarine because it can travel to where it is to operate under its own power. Travelling on the surface its radius is 400 nautical miles, and 35 nautical miles underwater, before the batteries need to be recharged. With a crew of four to six people, it can spend seven days at sea and has a life support system for another six days. The operational dive depth is 200 metres, although the customer can order a special version with an operational dive depth of 400 metres. The pressure hull is constructed from high-strength steel.

This design enables the submarine to undertake wide-ranging offshore operations such as the checking of pipelines or underwater cabling.

Inside, the internal space is divided up as follows: the engine room is in the stern. Forward of this is the compartment for equipment and supplies and the adjoining sanitary

A view of the upper deck with the snorkel mast collapsed (photo: Jörg Haas/BMT archive).

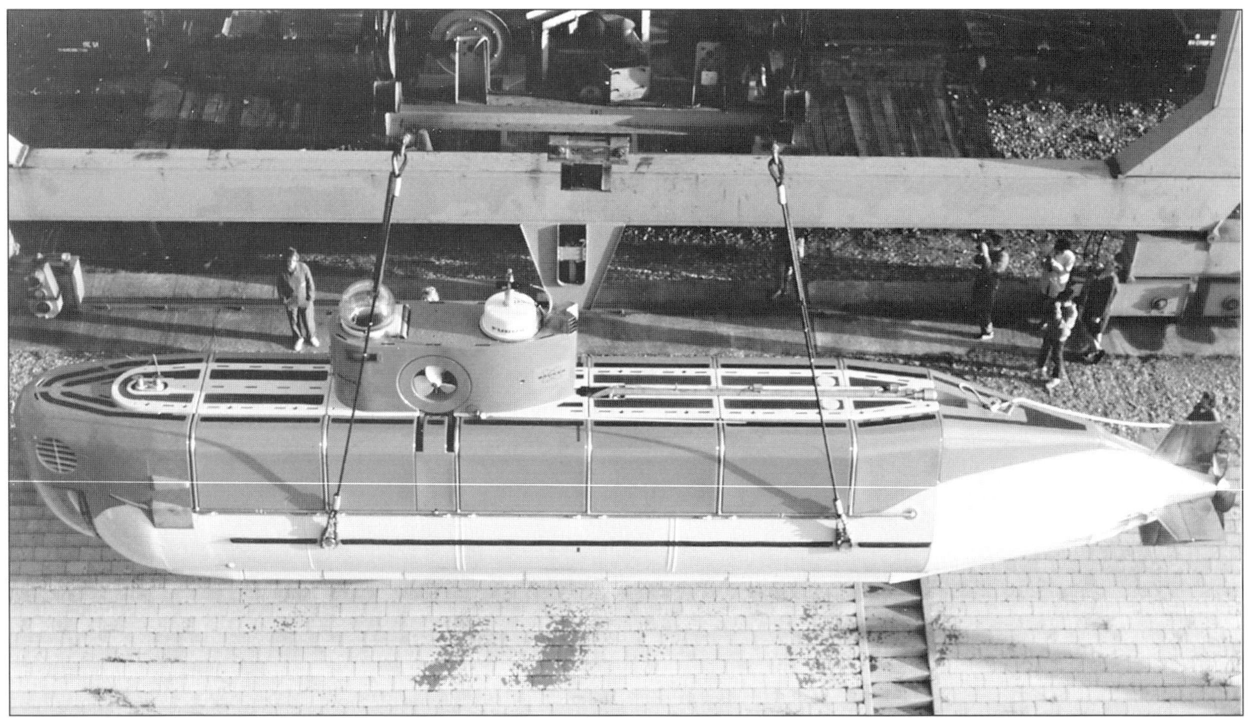

Above: Side view of the tower with its vertical swing propeller.

Left: The 'Seahorse's' steering and drive controls. Looking forwards at the back of the picture you can see the bow panorama window (photo: Jörg Haas/ BMT archive).

Above: View of the panoramic windowpane with its external protection

Above: Detailed view of the tower with entry dome (photo: Jörg Haas/BMT archive).

Left: The 'Seahorse's' stern with the cross rudder and the drive screw. In front, behind the protective mesh, is the stern jet propulsion.

unit. Then come the crew's combined sleeping and living quarters, also including a pantry. The command centre is located in the bow. The two pilots and a technician enjoy excellent vision through a round panorama window in the front of the bow. A brand new concept for submarine technology is fitted to the outside of this window: the 'Seahorse' has a screen cleaning system! If the submarine is operating on the sea bottom and the screen is dirtied by sediment or suchlike, all the pilot has to do is spray water onto the screen through high-pressure nozzles arranged in a circle around the screen and he has clear vision again.

The 'Seahorse' has a conventional propulsion system, using combined diesel/electric hydraulics. When surfaced, the diesel engine provides the propulsion and charges the accumulators. When submerged, the submarine is propelled electrically from the energy stored in the accumulators. The accumulators make up 25% of the submarine's total weight of 47.5 t.

The components that go to make up the 'Seahorse's' steering system are unique. In addition to the standard components: drive propeller, rudder and dive planes, the 'Seahorse' has a jet rudder on the bow and the stern. Two other swivel-mounted propellers on the tower enable the submarine to position itself and hover directly over its place of operation. All propulsion units work hydraulically and can be controlled from the command centre.

The internal and external flood and trim tanks are also controlled via the central hydraulic system. Both pilots can operate this system from the comfort of their seat in the command centre.

If the 'Seahorse' is equipped as an inspection submarine, it will have a selection of the following instruments:

Gyrocompass,
Autopilot,
Depth gauge,
Radio,
Underwater telephone,
An intercom system for external and on-board communication,
Sonar system,
Radar,
Pinger locator for distance measurements and object localisation,
Underwater video system with searchlights,
Gas analysis equipment to measure and monitor levels of O^2, CO^2, H^2,
Oxygen system,
Emergency breathing air supply, (BIB)
Barometer,
Hygrometer.

The modularity of this system facilitates the straightforward incorporation of equipment such as a scanning sonar, bottom profilers, manipulators, a drilling system and tools for non-diver applications. It is likewise possible to use ROVs (remote operated vehicles).

Further design plans for new versions were to include a diver exit and a version with a separate decompression chamber. Three 'Seahorses' were built. One of these incorporated a diesel propulsion system to operate independently of external air supply (re-circulation diesel engine). However, Bruker then withdrew from the market and transferred its business activities to HAUX LIFE SUPPORT. Whilst it appears that the era of work submarines is over, the unique know-how gained in this area lives on. The LULA research submarine was a product of this know-how, as were further developments that HAUX has made, for example, in the life support systems of the two 'Mir' submarines.

The 'Seahorse' to a scale of 1:10

Any model maker has every right to be proud if he succeeds in making a working model submarine that is an exact copy of the original. Yet, his pride is even more justified, if the model is so good that the company that manufactured the original wants to borrow his model to show at a trade fair.

This is what happened with Olaf Hantke's 'Seahorse'. Olaf Hantke is a member of the 'Cologne Friends of Model Submarines'. His model is built to a scale of 1:10. It was a real challenge, especially in terms of the potential of incorporating many special functions. The hull is 145 cm long, has a 23 cm beam and a height of 43 cm, including the tower. This meant a lot of work and demanded the application of new concepts of model construction.

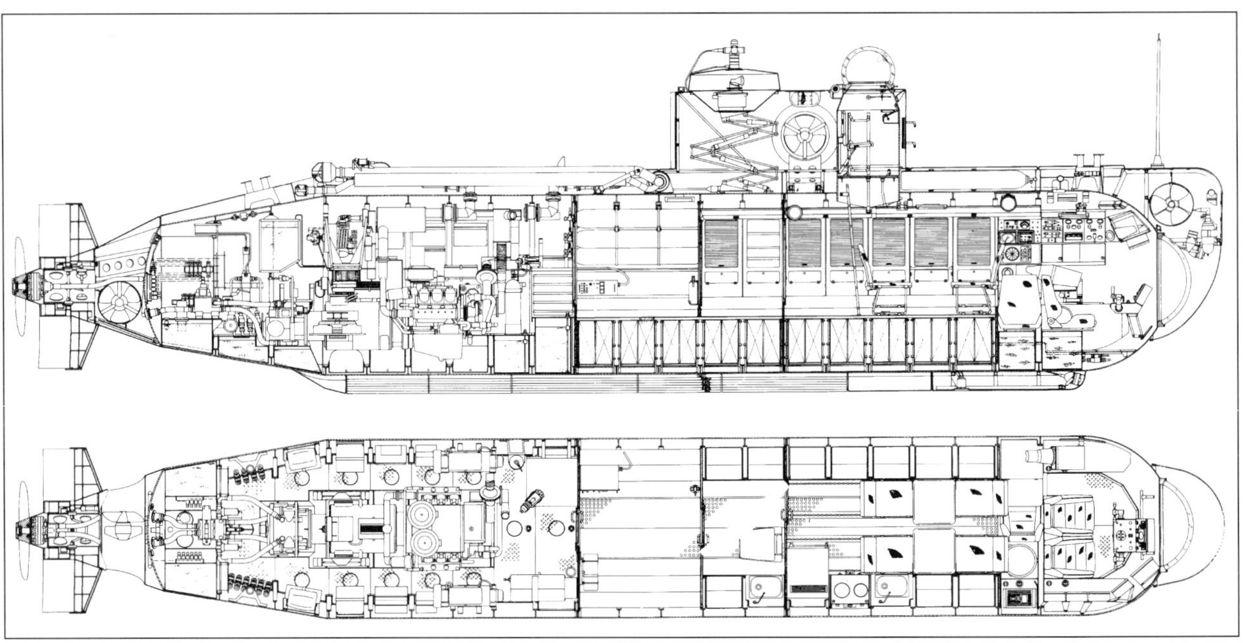

The 'Seahorse' in its home waters, the Fühlinger Lake in Cologne. The snorkel mast has already been raised, while the vertical propulsion systems and radar concertina mast are just being activated. At the front on the bow you can see the raised UKW aerial (photo: Norbert Brüggen).

The GRP hull was built from a mould provided by Rudi Schwarzmeier, who himself has one of the existing 'Seahorse' models.

The model consists of two sections. The first section is the hull. It is sealed by a Plexiglas lid and contains the diving, propulsion and remote control equipment. The second is the submarine's removable upper deck. The real challenge was to create the front panorama window and its bow protection. The internal, half-hemisphere shaped, pressure-tight window was deep drawn. The external protection was also deep drawn from 3 mm thick polycarbonate using a specially constructed aluminium form. The material is sufficiently robust to withstand the odd 'accident'.

To get such a big submarine with a correspondingly large internal volume to dive requires a little more effort. Olaf Hantke incorporated two systems. The submarine's main tanks comprise two tanks, each with a volume of two litres, and an 800 ml trim tank. Instead of a compressed air or piston-tank system Olaf Hantke chose to use laughing gas. A pressure container in the hull was used to hold 80 g of this gas in liquid form. The gas is pumped into or evacuated from the tanks by means of three rotary pumps. It requires 2 grams of gas to completely fill the tank.

More precise control of the submarine when submerged, including a hover function, is achieved by a second system, consisting of a piston tank with a volume of 400 ml. The tank is regulated by an automatic hover control developed by SONAR member, Helmuth Huhn.

It is also no mean thing to propel a weight of 42 kg. A 25-watt Faulhaber bell-armature motor is used as the drive motor and it turns a five-blade, 120 mm screw.

Like the original, the model 'Seahorse' has a lateral jet rudder on the bow and the stern, each having a capacity of 13 watts. These enable the model to turn on the spot or travel sideways.

This fantastic model has another highlight: the vertical propulsion system in the tower. There are two propeller units, each driven by a specially constructed Faulhaber type 17/20 motor with a 2 mm shaft, mounted beneath the deck. They can be raised by means of threaded control rods and levers and the whole system is powered by NiCd 12 volt/11 Ah batteries.

The very nature of the original gives the model maker the opportunity to really 'push the boat out' with a model of this scale and add creativity to the standard steering functions of rudder and dive planes. In the section about the propulsion system it has already been mentioned how the vertical motors can be raised. In addition to this, this 'Seahorse' can also raise the snorkel mast and radar mast as well as the FM aerial. These functions are likewise powered by motors with threaded control rods and levers.

The transmitter for the video camera is located in the snorkel mast; the camera itself is installed behind the bow window. A complete nautical illumination and three underwater searchlights in the bow, all made from the small head of Maglite torches, complete the model's special functions. All these special functions are connected by means of waterproof plugs on the Plexiglas cover and controlled via a decoder built into the hull.

Comex 'Remora 2000' – Panoramic view of the Deep

The Original

One of the most fascinating research submarines is the

'Remora 2000'. It was built in 1994 by the French group 'COMEX', based in Marseille. This group also operates the vessel. From its beginning up to 2001, it had built a total of 26 manned underwater vehicles.

The key design feature of the 'Remora 2000' is the way the pressure hull is built from transparent acrylic glass, to give the pilot and one observer an uninterrupted 300° view.

Left: The model with the upper deck removed. Under the beautifully detailed upper deck you can see one of the waterproof plugs. In the background Olaf Hantke is just making the last adjustments to the hull and the transmitter, before the 'Seahorse' glides into the depths of the Ihlow Sea near Aurich.

The 'Seahorse' on its stand. You can clearly see the two openings at the bow and the stern for the lateral jet rudders. Another noticeable feature is the sphere-shaped raised access hatch on the tower in front of the radar (photo: Norbert Brüggen).

The submarine has Bureau Veritas classification. It is approved to an operational dive depth of 610 metres, even though the acrylic glass sphere is manufactured to safely withstand a depth four times greater.

The submarine is 3.40 m long, 2.40 m wide and 2.15 m high.

Its total weight is 5.3 t and it is powered by five electro/hydraulic, encapsulated propeller drives with a diameter of 450 mm.

The submarine's steering system is computer controlled. All relevant parameters are communicated to the crew via a LCD flat screen. This means that the pilot can control the vessel without having to concentrate on operating each individual drive.

A moveable joystick box is used to steer the craft, with the pilot operating the functions of forwards/backwards and left/right with his right hand on the joystick. He uses his left hand to move a little turn wheel, which controls the submarine's vertical movement. The functions are further simplified by an automatic course and depth controller.

The 'Remora' on the A frame of the mother ship 'Minibex' (photo from Ingo Vollmer/Marlin Tauchservice www.marlin.de).

Similarly there is also an automatic hover function. This enables the submarine to pick up samples or loads when underwater, without affecting its position in the water, i.e. depth or pitch.

The 'Remora 2000' is equipped with a manipulator arm of the type Cybernetix SAMM5, which can be operated fully proportionally by the co-pilot or observer.

Three cameras are used to provide pictures. Two operate from the front: a swivel-mounted, colour video camera, which has a light sensitivity of 0.2-0.3 Lux, and an extremely sensitive black/white 0.001 lux camera that is used when visibility is poor.

To control what is going on at the back of the submarine there is a colour camera on the stern.

However, even the best cameras are not much use without the corresponding lighting. Consequently, the submarine has four high performance quartz halogen headlights and two HMI searchlights.

On this submarine operational safety is paramount. Should the submarine no longer be able to rise to the surface using the propulsion units, the pilot has the possibility of jettisoning 105 kg of lead ballast and activating an inflatable buoyancy vessel. These will bring the submarine back to the surface.

The 'Remora 2000' to scale of 1:6

When he built his 'Remora 2000', Jean-Pierre Courvoisier, a member of the Miniflotte Rhone Alps model-making club in France, made a technically audacious dream become a reality.

The shell of the hull's middle and top sections. These parts are likewise made to be pressure resistant and will contain the diving tank, the drive batteries and the RC electronics (photo: Jean-Pierre Courvoisier).

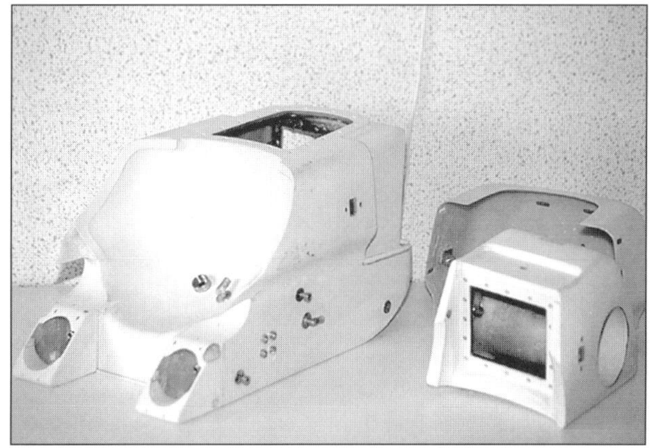

(Photo: Jean-Pierre Courvoisier).

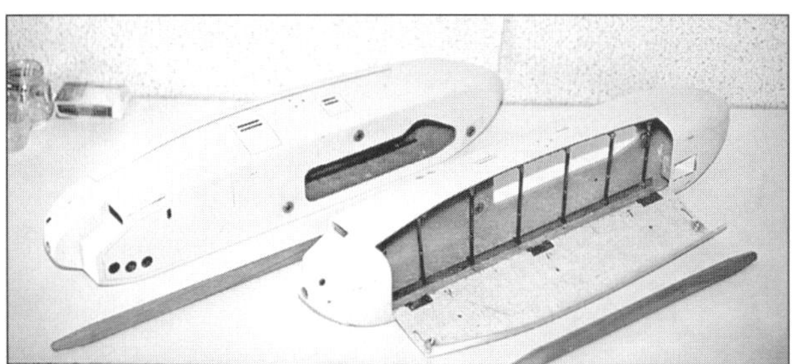

The finished floats with maintenance flap and reinforcements. The floats also contain the diving tanks (photo: Jean-Pierre Courvoisier).

The shell for the 'Remora's' internal section. This was made from PCB material, which was filled with plaster on the sides and sanded down to its rounded form. Careful planning was required to incorporate these components, since the external dimensions were greatly restricted by the opening in the sphere (photo: Jean-Pierre Courvoisier).

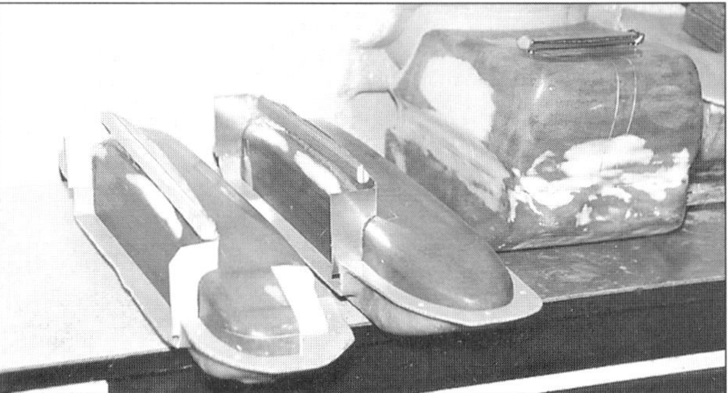

The 'Remora's' GRP hull sections were created with a multi-piece wooden mould. This picture shows the moulds for both the floats and the lower middle section. Before setting to work on his model, Jean-Pierre Courvoisier had the opportunity of measuring up the original (photo: Jean-Pierre Courvoisier).

Manufacturing the retainer section of upper ring lock from brass. The lid has a total diameter of 11 cm. The sphere is made from a special glass; it measures 28 cm in diameter and is attached to the lower section by M4 nuts and bolts (photo: Jean-Pierre Courvoisier).

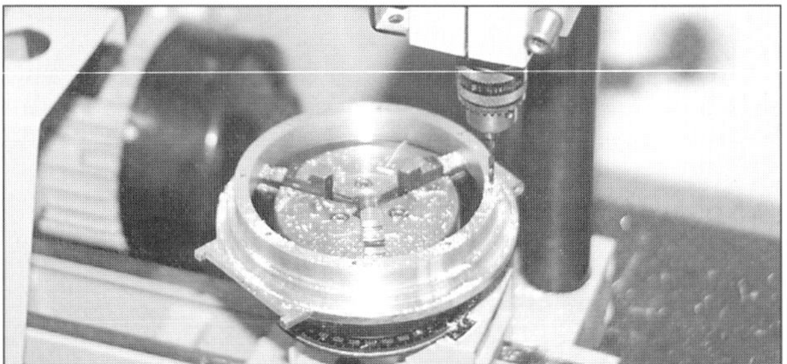

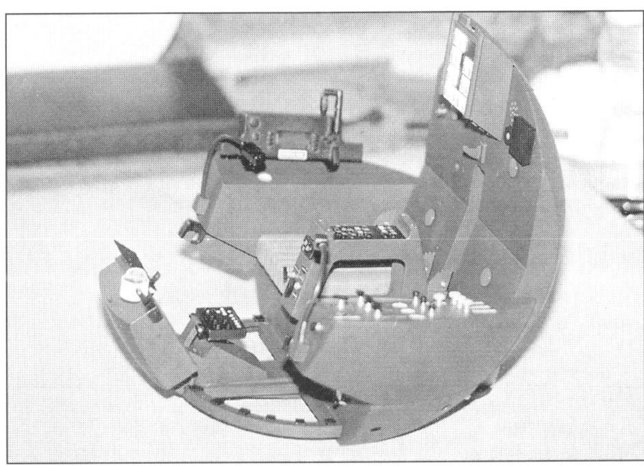

The finished internal section. All the switches and consoles are an exact replica of the original in both their appearance and the way they are lit (photo: Jean-Pierre Courvoisier).

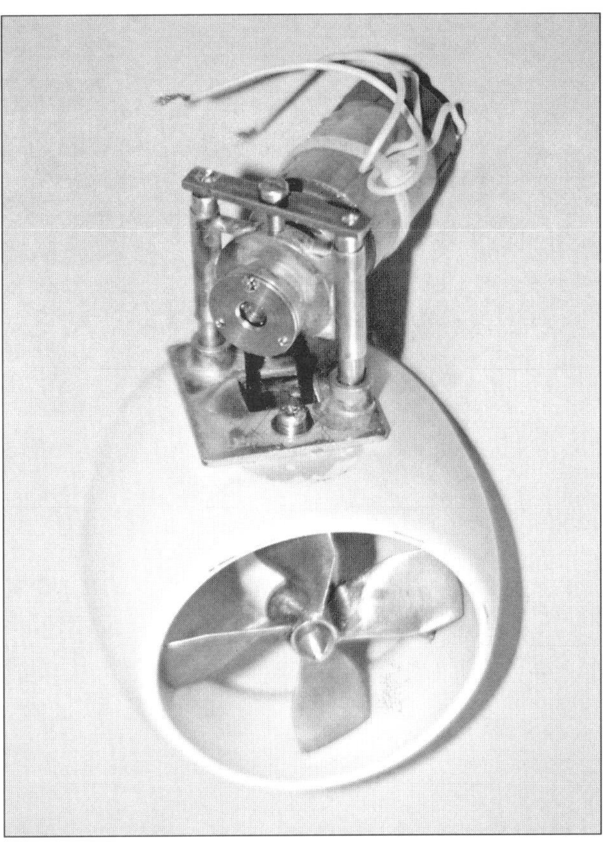

A view of one of the four propulsion thrusters. The space restrictions demanded that the components were mounted at an angle with a tooth belt transmission. All the components were made by hand, since it is almost impossible to obtain any suitable finished parts commercially (photo: Jean-Pierre Courvoisier).

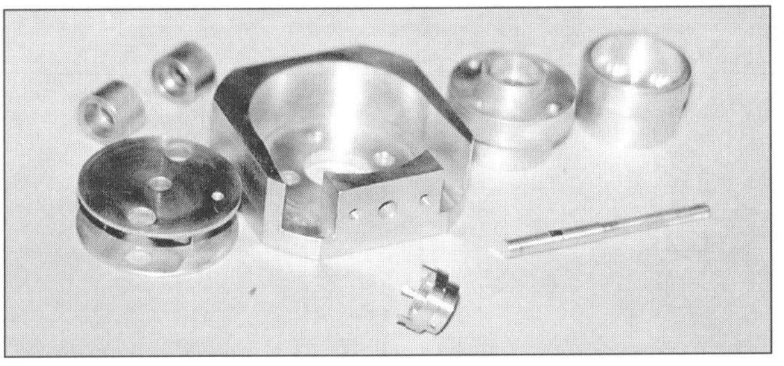

The mechanical parts of one of the two hose-pumps. The 'Remora 2000' dives with a system comprising several diving tanks. The hose pumps serve to flood the first tank with water, while the air from this tank is forced into other tanks and compressed (photo: Jean-Pierre Courvoisier).

The submarine successfully completed its initial diving trails in the safety of the indoor pool. A total of five propulsion thrusters make it extremely mobile. These are supplied by ten NiCad cells developing 4,000 mAh (photo: Jean-Pierre Courvoisier).

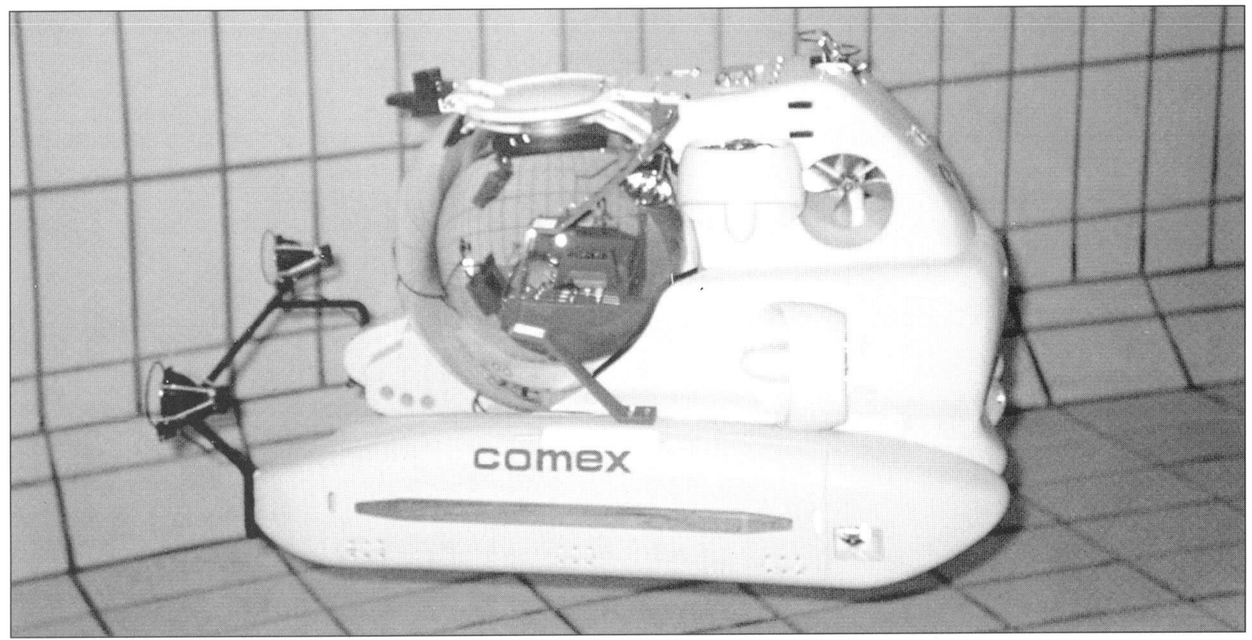

The finished components for the hull. Two diving tanks will later be mounted into each of the floats (photo: Jean-Pierre Courvoisier).

Most well known submarines and the models they inspire have a robustly configured pressure hull. In the model this either becomes part of the hull or is located inside the outer hull.

However, the 'Remora 2000' is different in this respect. A large part of the submarine consists of a transparent plastic sphere. This makes it all the more difficult to construct a model.

In the design stage it is necessary to undertake calculations with regard to pressure resistance and find a supplier for the sphere. In contrast to the original, the sphere in the model is not made from plastic, but was especially made from reinforced glass.

The internal contents of the sphere should replicate the original as exactly as possible. However the opening in the sphere restricts the size of the individual components.

The model took a long time to design and construct; the result is a real gem that replicates the detail of the original in almost every respect.

Jean-Pierre Courvoisier documented the construction on camera and provided the author with the pictures. Unfortunately it is not possible to show all the pictures, since this would go beyond the reach of this book. Nevertheless, it is hoped that the selection of photos included is sufficient to encourage you to also have a go at making submarines that are a bit out of the ordinary.

Left: The finished model of the 'Remora' – what a picture! The halogen headlights fitted to the bow have a capacity of 5 watts (photo: Jean-Pierre Courvoisier).

If you want to be the pilot of a research submarine, it is never too early to start. Kirsten and Joachim Jakobsen, managers of the foundation with their daughter Anna in front of the 'Lula' (copyright Rebikoff Niggeler Foundation).

Lula – Underwater perspective of the Azores

The Original

While military submarines are mass-produced, research submarines, on the other hand, are one-off constructions which are tailored to their application.

The research submarine 'Lula' of the Rebikoff-Niggeler Foundation, under the management of Kirsten and Joachim Jakobsen, is currently one of the newest examples.

The submarine is based at Horta, the headquarters of the foundation on the island of Faial in the Azores.

The technology used on the 'Lula' represents a milestone in the construction of research submarines. This sets the 'Lula' apart from its contemporaries.

Its mode of operation combines high tech with ecological aspects such as the use of a hybrid diesel/electric propulsion. The diesel engine is environmentally friendly and runs on vegetable oil.

The foundation provided the author with a presentation

(Copyright Rebikoff Niggeler Foundation).

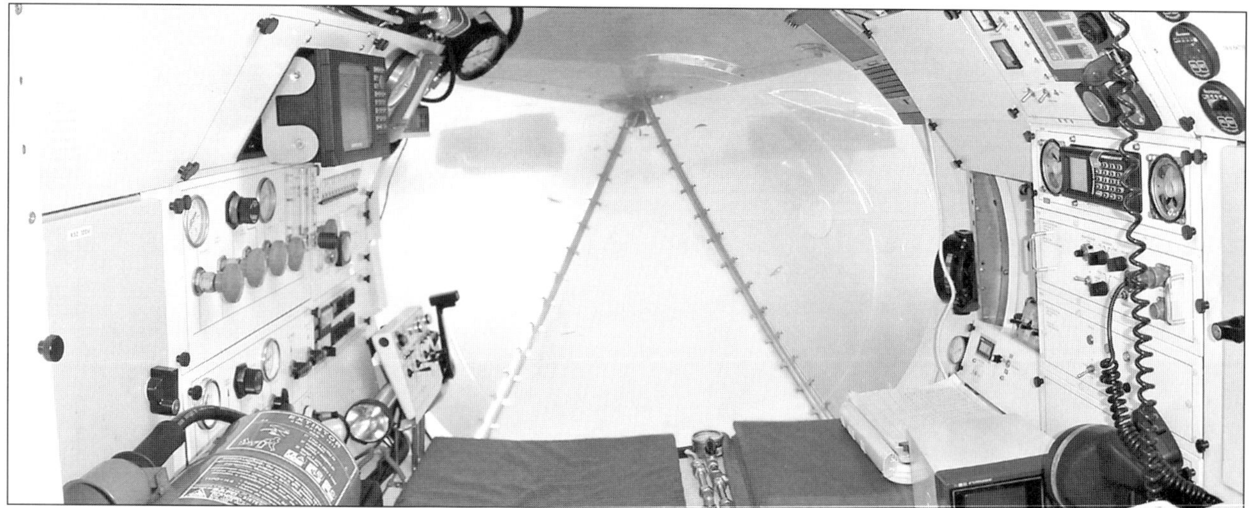

View forwards down the pressure hull through to the panoramic window. The submarine is steered from the left-hand seat (copyright Rebikoff Niggeler Foundation).

A view towards the stern down the pressure hull. The vegetable oil diesel engine unit can be seen in the stern (copyright Rebikoff Niggeler Foundation).

(Copyright Rebikoff Niggeler Foundation).

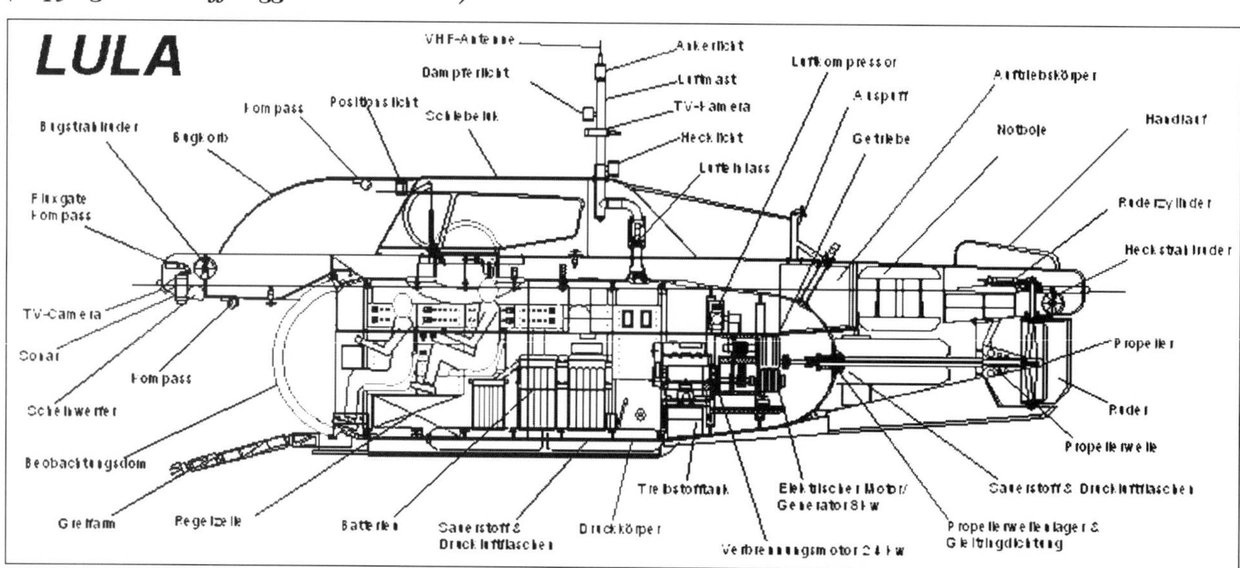

that summarises the technical data relating to the submarine, together with its capabilities and assignments. Anyone wishing to know more about this interesting submarine and what the foundation does are recommended to visit the foundation's home page at www.rebikoff.org

The Rebikoff Niggeler Foundation

Kirsten Jakosen

Fundação Rebikoff Niggeler, FRN, is a charitable foundation based on the island of Faial in the Azores. It is concerned with the documentation of the undersea world by film, photos and reports. It was founded in 1994 and in 2000 was given charitable status by the autonomous Azorian government.

The FRN also sees itself as a partner to other marine scientific institutions, with whom it draws up and carries out common projects. It intends to establish a centre of learning in the port of Horta (including: aquariums, the 'Lula' submarine with workshop, profundarium, laboratory, foundation headquarters, exhibition of underwater technology as well as film editing).

The FRN is the lifetime work of Dimitri and Ada Rebikoff Niggeler, who have been involved principally with the invention and development of technologies for undersea research and are known worldwide for their pioneering work in this area.

Between 1947 and 1950 Dimitri Rebikoff developed the portable electronic flash and the colour meter. He continued between 1950 and 1954 in developing different kinds of underwater camera (Stereofoto, 16 mm film, TV), the 'Pegasus' diver transporter, the remote controlled 'chien plongeur' and the 'Jonah'.

The Azores is a group of islands that have a volcanic origin and lie on the mid-Atlantic ridge in the North Atlantic. They offer easy access to the ocean for research.

The semi-autonomous submarine called 'Lula' (Portuguese for 'squid') was designed to facilitate scientific research in both coastal and oceanic regions. The vessel can dive to a depth of 500 metres and has space for the pilot and two other people.

A 150° panorama window with a diameter of 1.5 m enables the underwater world to be observed and recorded on film. It meets the classification and construction regulations of the American Bureau of Shipping (ABS) and is approved by the Seamen's Accident Prevention and Insurance Association in Hamburg.

The air-conditioning and safety systems are regulated by micro-processor controlled electronics. A modern navigation system enables precise navigation. Position, course and depth are processed digitally by a computer and also logged on a map plotter.

Samples up to a weight of 25 kg can be taken off the seabed by means of a mobile grab-arm. A photo and video camera is mounted on the head of the manipulator arm, as well as an electronic flash and spotlights. For scientific work there is a wide range of pre-installed sensors and samplers. A film camera incorporated in the focal point of the dome provides pictures of the undersea world.

When travelling from the port to the dive area, a KPM-Lombardini 24 kW engine enables a speed of 6 knots. This runs on 100% vegetable oil.

A compressor fills the compressed air tanks and a motor/generator charges the batteries. Electric horizontal and vertical motors provide maximum manoeuvrability in all three axes.

The 'Lula' submarine research assignments

Biology: Benthos (sea-bed) and Pelagial (open water):
Study and documentation of the biocoenoses,
Comparison of the islands and the undersea mountains,
Collection of organisms for behavioural, physiological and ecological study etc,
Study of the squid that inhabit the Azores,
Investigation of the biocoenses at hydrothermal sources.

Geology:
Cartographical elevation and observation of structures,
Investigation of hydrothermal and other volcanic activities,
Collection of rock samples,
Measurement of gravitational and magnetic fields.

Sea mammals:
Observation and study of the whales and dolphins that inhabit the Azores.

Oceanographic measurements:
Oxygen content,
Salt content,
Temperature,
Conductivity.

Environmental protection:
Water sampling,
Determination of the effects of pollution.

Fishing:
Analysis of fish stocks (for the setting of catch quotas),
Inspection of long-line fishing.

Shipwrecks and undersea structures:
Search and location,
Inspection and documentation,
Cartographic record.

Address:
Fundação Rebikoff Niggeler
Rocha Vermelha,
Praia do Almoxarife,
P-9900 Horta
Faiai
Açores
Portugal
Tel: (+351) 292-949 505
Fax: (+351) 292-949 563
www.rebikoff.org
rebikoff@sapo.pt

Technical data – 'Lula'

Manufacturer:	
Pressure hull	Overlasko, NL
Dome	Stanley Plastics, GB
Deck and shaft system	MSL, Plymouth
Systems	Haux Life Support
Class index	ABS Europe XA1
Nominal dive depth	500 m
Test depth	630 m
Destruction depth	1,000 m
Complement	one pilot, two passengers
Total length	8.50 m
Width	1.65 m
Height	2.65 m
Displacement	9.3 t
Diving tanks	1,100 litre
Variable ballast	Water, 200 litre
Oxygen supply	3 x 27 litre, 200 bar
Air supply	5 x 27 litre, 200 bar
Propulsion on water	KPM-Lombardini, 24 kW 3,600 revs/min.
Propulsion underwater	electric 1 x 8 kW, 4 x 5 kW.
Emergency buoy	1,700 m, 12 mm dyneema cable.
Observation window	1,450 mm diameter, 150°
Entry hatch	540 mm diameter, 150°
Ballast jettison	110 kg, hydraulically
Communication	10 kHz, 27 kHz and VHF
Batteries	1 x 120V/180A, 2 x 24V/ 160A, 1 x 12V/60A
Navigation	Notebook, echo sounder, map-plotter, sonar, fluxgate compass, log, depth-gauge, 3-D navigation software
Cameras	s/w navigation camera, colour video camera, photo camera
Lighting	7 x 500 W
Electronic flash	2,100 W/sec
Grab arm	25 kg, five functions.

The 'Lula' does not need its own mother-ship, only an accompanying rubber dinghy approximately 5 m in length to maintain communication. This lack of complexity in its practical use makes it possible for the first time to undertake a wide range of small and large research and film projects.

Numerous dives in Azorian waters have already yielded rare pictures of animals as never seen before in their natural habitat.

The 'Lula' to a scale of 1:10

With his model of the 'Seahorse' Olaf Hantke from the 'Cologne Friends of Model Submarines' had already succeeded in building one unusual and seldom seen model.

You can use exactly the same words to describe his next project. His model of the 'Lula' to a scale of 1:10 is 85 cm long. The submarine's pressure hull consists of a plastic tube, 15.3 cm in diameter and 45 cm long. The upper section was created from GRP mouldings that are free flooding.

The diving system involves a double hose pump with a Maxon motor, which takes 40 seconds to fill or empty a 1.35 litre diving tank made from pool liner material.

The remote control components are the ones that are normally used in tube type module constructions, these are mounted onto an equipment frame.

The propulsion components are powered by 12V/4,000 mAmp NiMH batteries.

As is the case with the 'Seahorse', a highlight of the model is the propulsion system. In additional to the main propulsion, which incorporates a 25 watt Maxon motor located in the stern, driving a 52 mm three-blade screw, the submarine has front and rear lateral jet rudders as well as two vertical rudders which are located next to the tower. This propulsion configuration makes the submarine exceptionally manoeuvrable.

The 'Lula' is equipped with four searchlights, which are arranged in vertical pairs and point forwards. This is in addition to full nautical illumination.

A look inside the opened bow cockpit. You can clearly see the arrangement of batteries and the hose connections of the diving pump (photo: Norbert Brüggen).

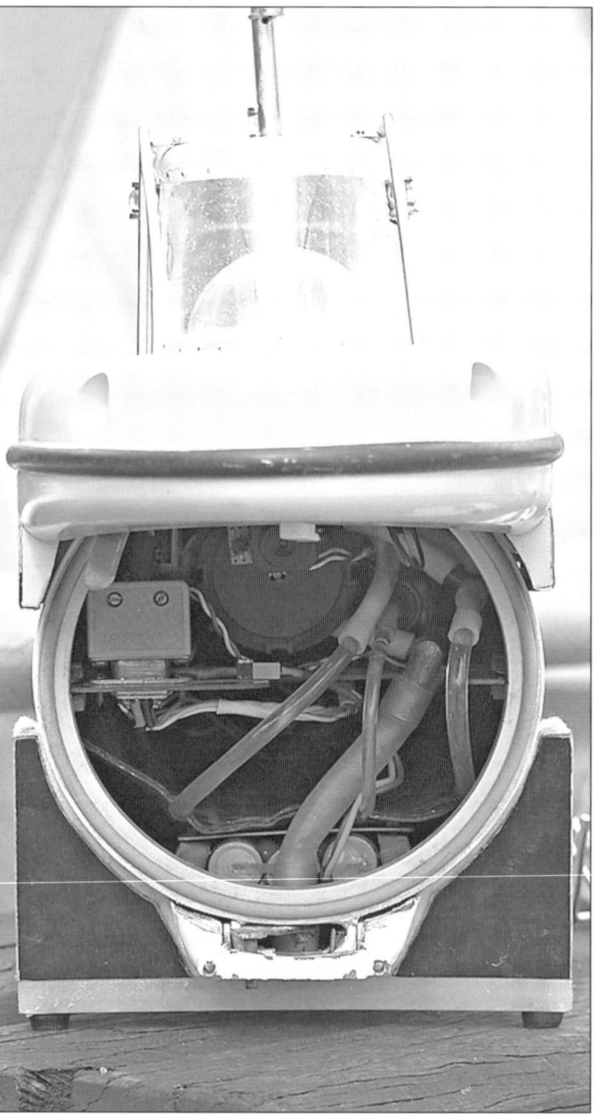

The 'Lula' on its stand. This clearly shows the proportions of the pressure hull in relation to the upper section. The photo was taken before the first maiden voyage and some parts of the submarine are yet to be painted (photo: Norbert Brüggen).

The front view of the submarine when travelling on the surface. The curved railings also protect the superstructure (photo: Norbert Brüggen).

From this perspective it is hard to spot the difference between the model and the original (photo: Norbert Brüggen).

The bow glazing equates to a pressure hull diameter of 15.3 cm and makes it very easy to install a camera (photo: Norbert Brüggen).

'Stint' – Helmut Walter's Vision

The Original

In 1967 Helmut Walter designed the deep-sea diving boat he called the 'Stint'. At that time the concepts he used were far ahead of their time and surpassed all previously known designs. Unfortunately, the application of rather complex technical solutions and the use of raw materials that had not previously been tested proved to be a major handicap. The result was that, in spite of the uniqueness of his work, he was unable to find someone willing to buy his submarine.

(Drawing: Carsten Standfuß archive)

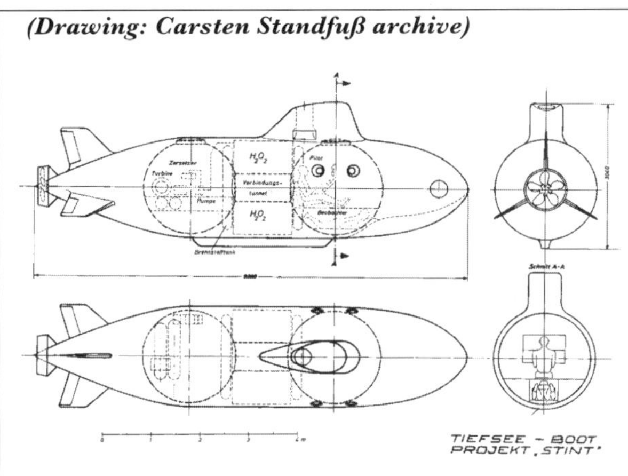

Technical data:

Length	9 m
Height with tower	3.04 m
Total displacement	24 tons
Propulsion	37 kW Walter turbines exchange method with or without combustion chamber, diesel
Fuel reserve	3,000 kg H_2O_2 (hydrogen peroxide)
Propulsion and speed properties	cold method (non-fuel burning) 350 nm at 5 knots Hot method (fuel burning) 750 nm at 5 knots or 200 nm at 10 knots
Maximum dive depth	1,000 metres

The main propulsion comes from a turbine powered stern screw, which is mounted in a kort-nozzle. Three rudder surfaces are arranged in a star configuration in front of the propulsion to provide rudder and dive plane steering. To increase the manoeuvrability, a bow jet rudder is fitted. Also a vertical thruster with encapsulated electric motors can be found in the submarines central section. The submarine has a particularly streamlined shape. Internally it consists of two pressure-resistant steel spheres, each with a diameter of 2 metres. The front sphere contains the drive and observation controls for the crew of two. The propulsion system is mounted in the rear sphere with turbine, decomposer and pump. The H_2O_2 required is stored above and below the tunnel joining the two spheres.

The pilot sits in the sphere. He can see through four small portholes that look out on the port and starboard sides of the sphere. The observer lies in the lower section of the sphere with one porthole to see forwards and downwards.

The 'Stint' to a scale of 1:10

SONAR member Heinrich Kistenich was very interested in Helmut Walter's 'Stint' design. So much so, that working together with his son, he brought it to life to a scale of 1:10. The result is a fascinating model, which very clearly shows the operational capabilities of the planned original.

In the chosen scale the model is 900 mm long, has a diameter of 210 mm and a weight of 24 kg.

It was built according to the drawing (left), whereby the dimensions were converted onto graph paper. The submarine and all the necessary systems were designed from the inside out. Starting with the middle ring lock, this was over laminated with polystyrene sheet and when removed, it formed the shape of the hull. The tower was created from a plywood mould.

The diving system consists of a scratch-built 1,000 ml piston diving tank, which is located centrally on the equipment frame. The diving system also has to include a method of controlling pitch and depth, so as to be able to adjust the submarine's horizontal position and its dive depth.

The equipment frame is fixed to the back bayonet lock. For maintenance, however, it can be folded down 90° on to the propulsion and rudder system. Each of the three rudders is driven directly by a servo with counter gears. The Y-configuration of the rudder requires a special steering mechanism. Consequently, the rudders are controlled by a mixer.

The 'Stint' surfacing.

The 'Stint's' equipment frame with the front section removed.

The Y-rudder configuration and a view of the front hull section. In the foreground you can see the tower that has been removed with the cut-out for the central jet thruster.

When the model travels in a curve, it also counteracts the tendency of the model to lean.

The main drive motor has an operating voltage of 14.4 volts. The other components of the propulsion system include the lift-propeller in the tower and the stern jet rudder which are both permanently fixed into the hull. At about the height where in the original the observer can look out of the submarine, there is a 12-volt halogen spotlight. This is strongly built and carefully mounted to protect it against springing a leak should it hit the bottom.

The drive motor, dive pump, the two auxiliary drives and the halogen spotlight are supplied with sufficient voltage from a total of 36 cells developing 4,000 mAh, which are located in three battery packs. This results in a total capacity of 12 ampere hours, which are theoretically sufficient for full throttle on the propulsion motor for 1.5 hours. However, since the model is only rarely driven at full speed, the actual travel time of the model is considerably longer.

The 'Stint' is equipped with other refinements, which indicate how well thought through the design is. This is clearly evidenced by some of the following examples:

The keel runner contains an adjustable, lead ballast. This makes it possible to achieve a correct trim without any further alterations to the model.

The bow jet rudder is coupled with a side rudder, but it is switched in such a way that it is not driven when the submarine is in motion.

A plug coupling is built into the main ring lock; this automatically establishes an electrical connection as soon as the front hull section is locked to the stern.

The receiver system is switched in such a way that when the transmitter signal fails, the submarine automatically surfaces.

A lighting system with its own electricity supply ensures that the model can be seen even in murky waters.

A water sensor in the tower ensures that the lift jet rudder is only electrically actuated when the model is operated in water.

Further details can be added to this list, yet they would go beyond the scope of this article. Since it was completed in 1996 Heinrich Kistenich's submarine has dived 167 times, completing around 500 operational hours (status February 2003).

'Alvin' – Pioneer of the deep

The Original

The 'Alvin' belongs to the US Navy. It is operated by the Woods Hole Oceanographic Institute and is certainly the most well known research submarine. It came into service in 1964 and has continually been improved. It is one of the very few submarines with a current operational dive depth of 4,500 metres. Fame came to the submarine in 1966, when off the coast of Spain it found a hydrogen bomb that had been lost in an aircraft collision.

Later the submarine was repeatedly associated with new deep-sea discoveries or with spectacular dives such as those to the wreck of the 'Titanic' with the man who discovered it, Dr. Robert D. Ballard.

Technical data	
Length	7.10 m
Height	3.70 m
Width	2.60 m
Gross weight	17 t
Operational dive depth	4,500 metres
Pressure hull	diameter of 2.08 m made from 4.9 cm thick titan steel.
Payload	680 kg
Propulsion	Six thuster drives using 35 kWh. 46.8 kWh. maximum.
Maximum range	5 km
Speed	Cruise speed 0.8 km/h, max. 3.5 km/h
Normal operational duration	6-10 hours
Life support systems	216 hours
Complement	One pilot, two scientists.

The 'Alvin' on its way to the deep (source NOOA).

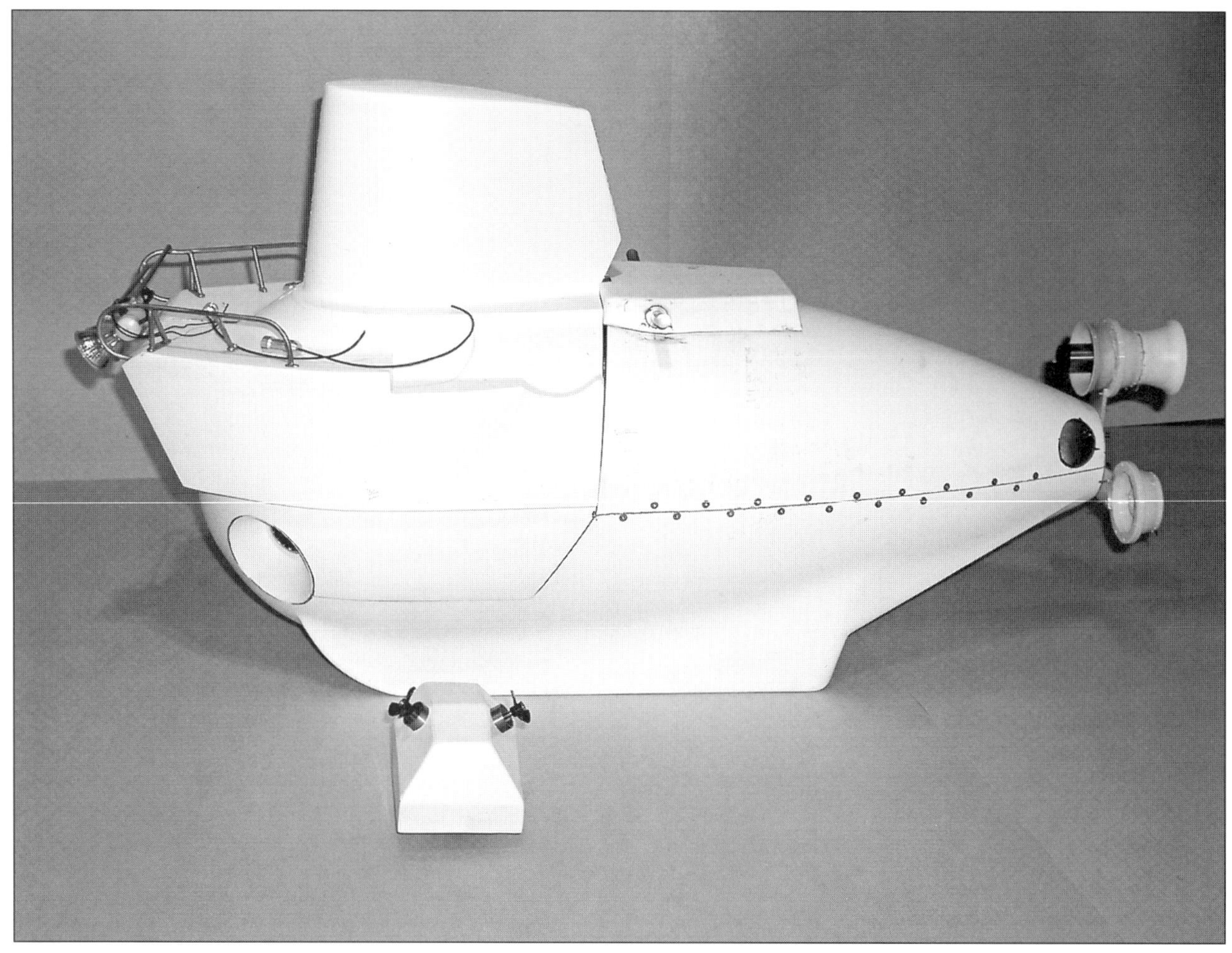

Side view of the shell of the 'Alvin', in front, the ROV 'Jason Junior'. You can see the mounts for the thrusters on the stern, the top one is complete apart from the motor cover. The struts located behind the tower are the shafts of the tower thrusters.

The 'Alvin' is of modular design and can be equipped according to the particular assignment. For visual work there is comprehensive lighting system together with high-resolution cameras. In addition, it is also possible to attach different sample baskets to the bow, which can be filled with the help of the two manipulator arms. A bow basket will also hold a small ROV (remote operated vehicle). It is thanks to such a ROV that we have the spectacular photographs of the inside of the 'Titanic'.

'Alvin' and 'Jason Junior' to a scale of 1:8 Under construction

Submarines that do not come in kit form usually take much longer to build. If at the same time you are writing a book about model submarines and their originals, then there is hardly any time left for model-building at all. However, the 'Alvin' deserves a mention at this point, even though it is at present still 'under construction'.

Research submarines offer the model maker any number of creative possibilities that are withheld from those who make models of military submarines.

With a few exceptions, the availability of these submarines is restricted. After much research I found the 'Alvin' from FX Models in the USA.

This model was featured in the BBC series 'Nautilus' – History of Underwater Travel. In the film the model is not seen in anything close to its true element; instead it floats through a cloud chamber in order to suggest the infinite depth of the oceans.

Three months after I placed the order, it arrived as a rather expensive UPS package. It was subject to numerous taxes. In fact, in the end the initial price of 550 dollars for the Alvin hull was almost doubled. However, this submarine was to be something special. The hull was well packaged in a strong box and was the first model that FX had ever sent to Europe.

The package also contained instructions for building the model as conceived by FX. The propulsion system was to consist of a gearless Speed 700, driving a 14 cm large screw. One can add, somewhat ironically, that this configuration at least gives you a nice warm pool from the heat generated by the controller.

It is recommended that Graupner Seabex One drives are used for the tower thrusters and that these are controlled by flexible shafts. The RC-equipment and the drive motors should be stowed in a waterproof box. There are no plans to install a diving tank.

Whilst everyone has their own opinion, it appeared that all in all this construction concept did not really match the possible capabilities of the submarine. After quite a long time in the planning, a concept was developed of how the 'Alvin' should be equipped.

Shell sections of one of the three stern thrusters (photo Norbert Brüggen).

Detailed photograph of the upper section of the hull. The bracket for the halogen spotlight is fixed to the railing. Underneath this are the cut-outs for the three viewing windows. The Plexiglas for the windows has been turned to form a true-to-life shape and fitted with micro-screws. There is the option of fitting another light source behind the windows.

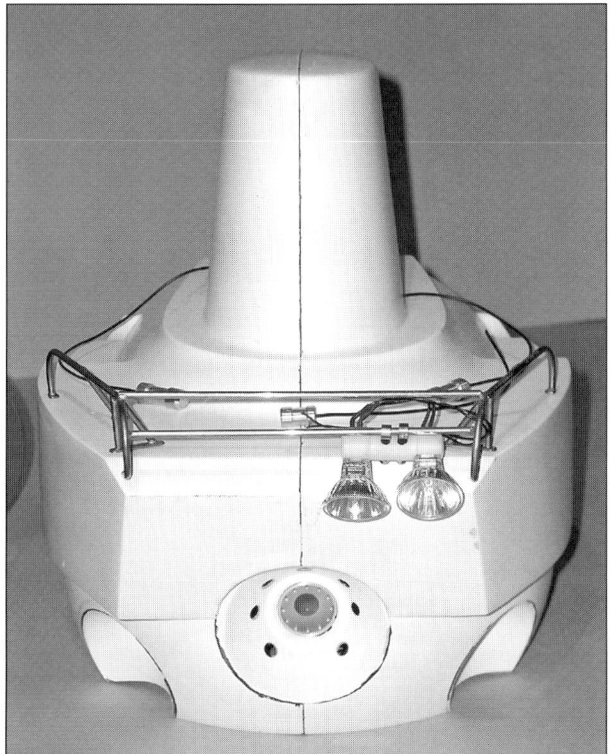

Basic components of the tower thrusters. The main body consists of two turned brass parts, one of which is inserted into the other and sealed with an O-ring. An oil seal is used to seal the motor shaft (photo Norbert Brüggen).

Photo of the bow of the 'Alvin' with the ROV, 'Jason Junior'. The ROV is subsequently parked on the submarine in a small bow basket garage, before it drives independently.

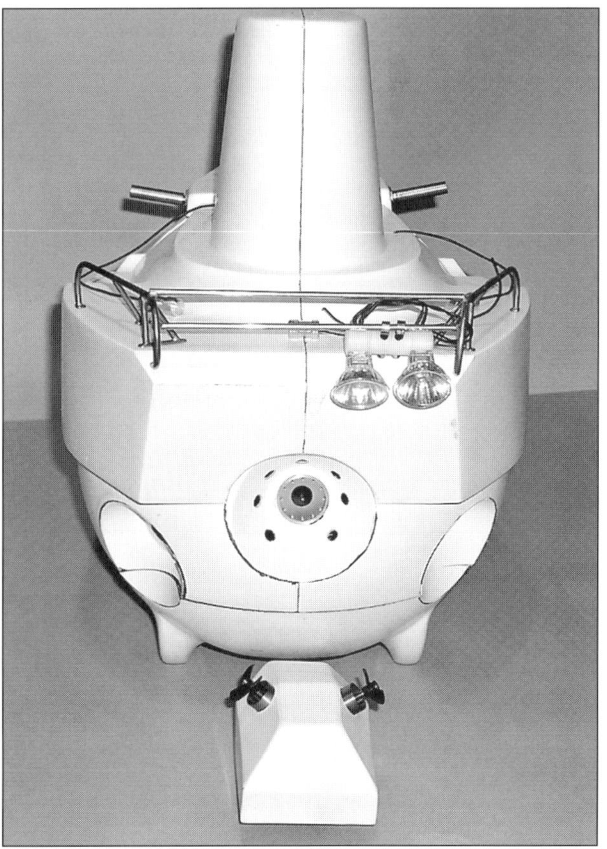

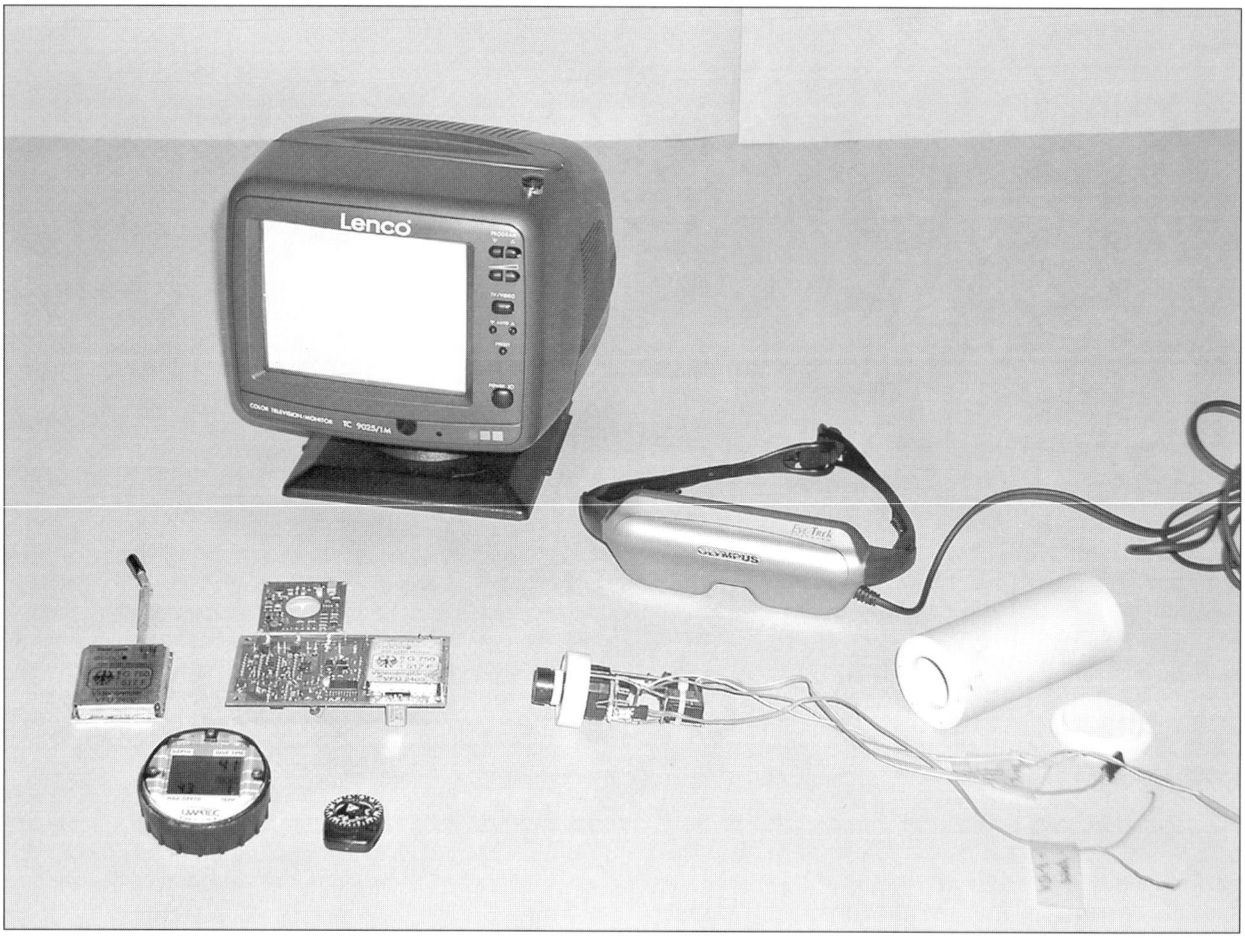

View of the 'Alvin's' videotelemetry. At the top the small colour TV; next to it, the video glasses. On the left in the middle, the video transmitter and the receiver; underneath, the dive computer and compass. On the right of the picture you can see the camera and the corresponding housing. All components are fitted in such a way that they can operate from batteries and independently of the network voltage.

The three main sections of the submarine. On the left the lower hull section with the inserted pressure hull; this has a variable fixing to adjust the submarine's pitch. In the middle, the equipment frame with the Engel diving tank fitted. On the right you can see the upper section of the hull.

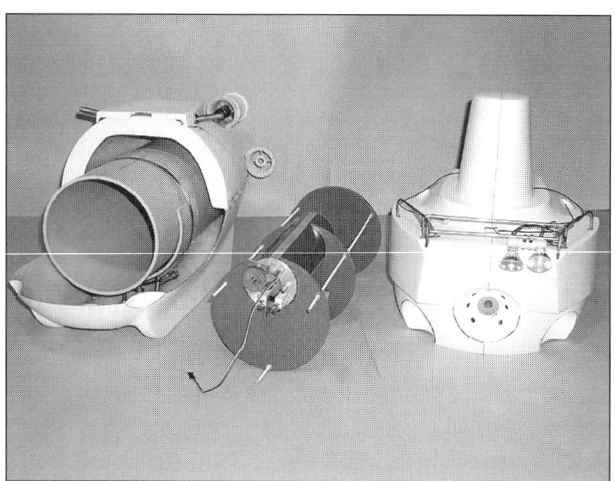

Detailed view of the submarine's stern. The stern jet rudder is mounted in the milled opening in front of the thrusters. When operational, the mounting for the three stern thrusters is covered by a semi-circular cover.

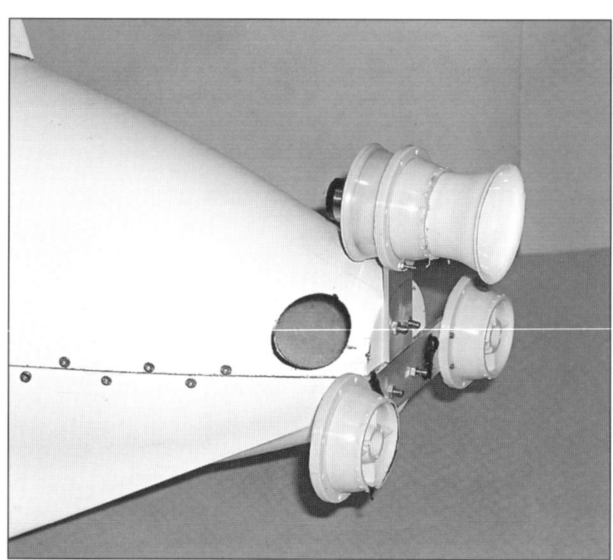

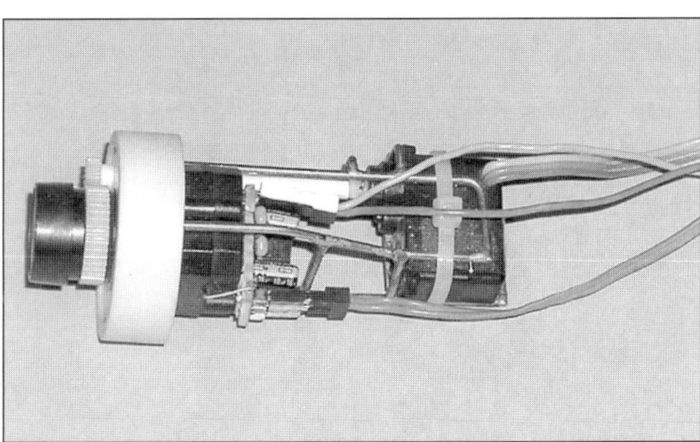

The 'Alvin's' camera. It is possible to sharpen the image underwater using a drive attachment on the focus and a converted drive control with a servo.

The core element of the submarine is a 180 mm PVC tube with a length of 430 mm. An equipment frame is mounted in the tube, containing all the diving and RC equipment. A 750 ml Engel piston tank is used as a ballast tank; it has a fully proportional, magnetically supported controller. While the FX version has a large drive propeller at the stern, equating to the submarine's previous design stage, the 'Alvin' is equipped with retro-fitted innerspace thrusters, such as are fitted today to the stern of the original. These are driven by Faulhaber bell-armature geared motors. The thruster prototypes were manufactured by 'Norbert Brüggen Modell-U-Boot-Spezialitäten'.

The conning tower thrusters are turned brass parts that likewise contain a Faulhaber motor. To give the submarine maximum manoeuvrability, each of the thrusters is actuated by a waterproof servo acting at 180°. The combination with the stern jet rudder creates drive capabilities similar to that of a helicopter.

As stated at the beginning, research submarines not only look interesting from the outside, they also captivate because they offer the possibility of special functions. The 'Alvin' is equipped with a full range of lights and a special camera system, for which, thanks to modeller colleague Richard Bünder, it is possible to adjust the focus/picture quality by remote control. The camera is contained in a separate housing and can be swivelled using a waterproof servo. In the normal position the camera points forward; if you use the servo to swivel it downwards, a dive computer appears in the picture giving the current depth and other values, together with a compass. The picture and sound signals are sent via a buoy to a receiver that, depending on the application, feeds a small colour TV or video glasses. Driving with video glasses is a real experience.

Two small LCD screens in the glasses create the impression of a two-metre large projection screen in front of your eyes. To illuminate the camera field, two 20-watt halogen spots are fixed in a mounting on the bow railing and additional lighting is provided by several ultra-bright, white LEDs.

The fact the original is modular in construction gives you free rein to add further functions. The combination of a compass and dive computer is just one possibility amongst many others, including the addition of other lighting and different bow baskets, like in the original.

Another interesting bow basket addition is a ROV together with its garage. To create an authentic, remote-controlled model of this ROV will certainly take time and is a considerable challenge.

URF – Rescue in a dire emergency

The Original

'A few hundred metres under the surface of the sea lies a submarine on the sea-bed, no longer able to resurface. Emergency supplies of electricity and air are being used; the main systems are damaged or have failed. Inside the submarine it is dark, except for a few lamps. The heating has likewise failed and the crew are freezing. Condensation is running down the walls; in the cold each breath appears as wisp of mist. It is getting harder to breathe. The crew are trapped in the deep. Water is coming in.

Umpteen submarines lie on the bottom of the sea, steel coffins as the result of a scenario, such as described above. There are very few survivors who live to tell their story. The number of such cases increased as submarines began to be used for military purposes. Today it is only possible to save yourself from a stricken submarine down to a depth of 80 metres. Older submarines did have their escape systems that enabled the crew to leave the submarine through an open hatch. In recent times, more modern rescue suits have made it safer to escape from vessels in a similar way.

Crew members that had escaped and made it to the surface were still far from safe. Survival was threatened by lung injuries due to excess pressure and the dangers of the open sea, should a rescue ship not be at hand. Today, submarines operate at much greater depths, making it impossible to exit freely.

The URF – submarine rescue system of the Royal Swedish Navy – was conceived by the Kockum shipyard and is built for the purpose of rescuing the crew directly from a stricken submarine. The Swedish Navy only operates conventionally propelled submarines which do not have the size of crew of a nuclear submarine. Consequently, the URF is designed to have a capacity to rescue the whole 35 crew of a submarine with one dive. The URF is supported by the mother ship 'Belos' which has sufficient medical facilities as well as pressure chamber capacity. However, the URF is not tied to its mother ship in principle. The submarine can be taken to any port by low-loader and work together with other suitable surface vessels.

Deployment involves the URF being taken to within a mile of the stricken craft; it is lowered into the sea and then dives. The stricken submarine is located by means of sonar and visual systems and the URF docks onto the rescue exit. The docking manoeuvre is possible up to an angle of 45° and a maximum deployment depth of 460 metres. Once the crew has successfully transferred from the stricken submarine, the URF returns to the surface and is taken back on board the mother ship.

Since its construction in 1976, the system's capability has been put to the test in many manoeuvres. The concept is so successful that a follow-up submarine is under construction.

Technical data

Total length	13.9 m
Width/height	3.20 m
Displacement	52 t
Propulsion	single shaft, electric/ hydraulic thrusters
Speed	3 knots
Maximum deployment depth	460 m
Underwater endurance	85 hours
Complement	3 crew
Rescue capacity	3t/35 people

(Copyright Kockum's).

The URF on the A-frame hoist of the 'Belos' (copyright Kockum's).

The 'Belos' – the URF's mother ship (photo: Volker Küster).

A view onto the upper deck (photo: Volker Küster).

Volker Küster, one of the builders of the URF model on the upper deck of the URF (photo: Volker Küster).

Stern view of the URF with cross rudder and kort-nozzle screw. The stern jet rudder is located behind the grid cover (photo: Volker Küster).

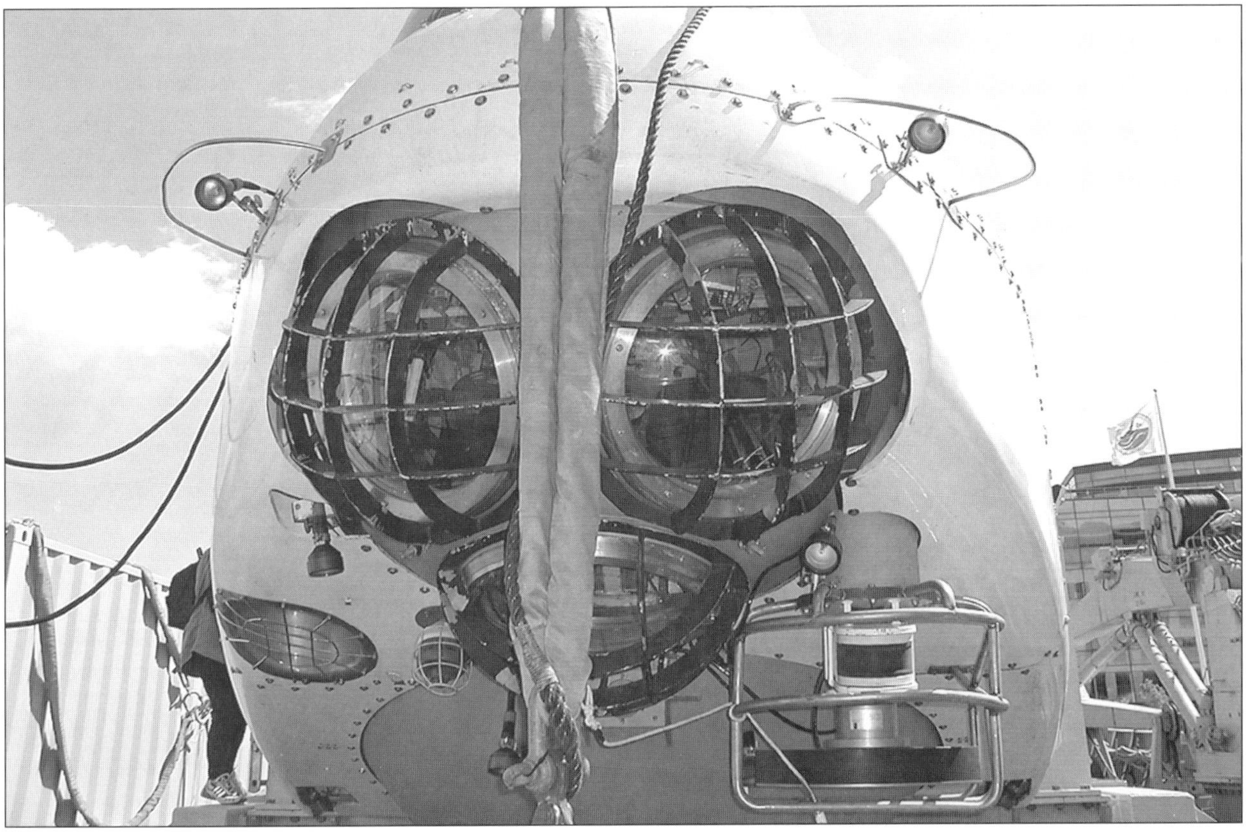

Bow view with the three portholes protected by metal sheilds (photo: Volker Küster).

A view from the pilot's seat. On the left and right you can see the joysticks used to steer the submarine (photo: Volker Küster).

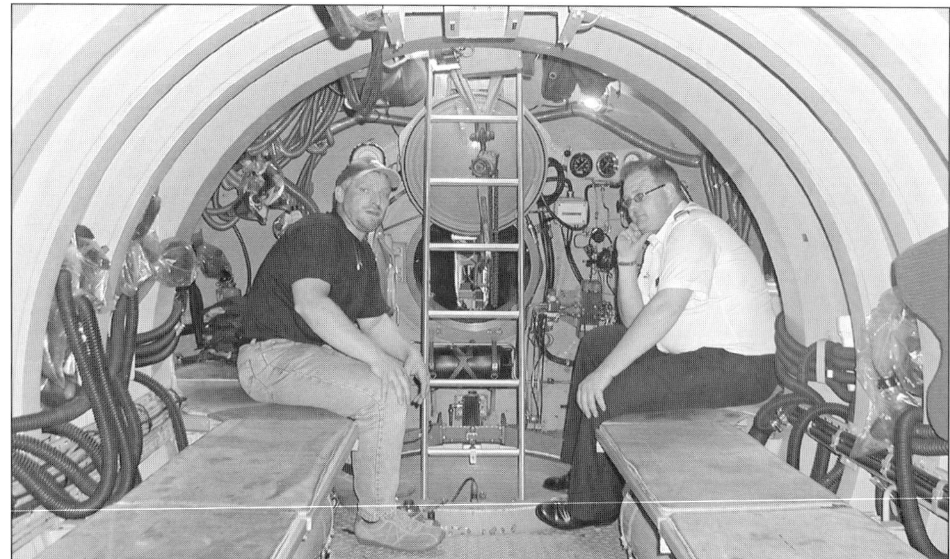

The URF's rescue compartment. If necessary this can accommodate 35 people or an enthusiastic modeller in conversation with the URF's on-board engineer (photo: Volker Küster).

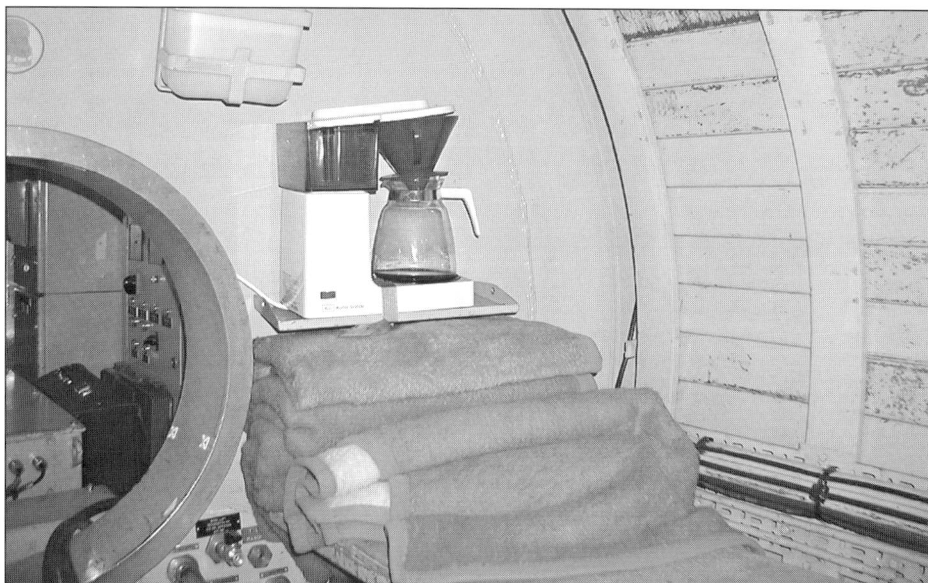

You should never be without – the coffee machine on board (photo: Volker Küster).

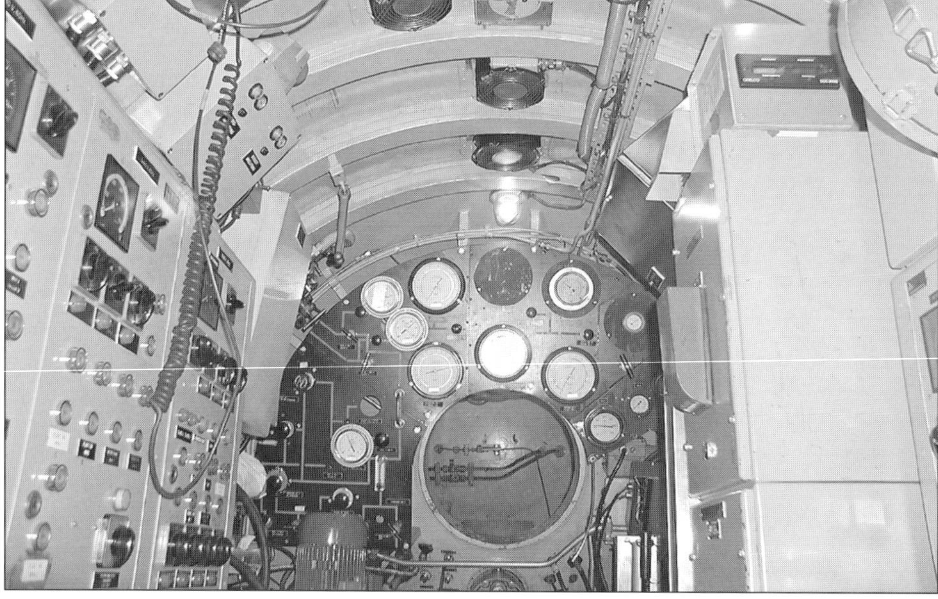

A part of the technical compartment on the URF (photo: Volker Küster).

The URF to a scale of 1:30

SONAR members Klaus Peter Hoffmann and Volker Küster have worked together to develop the first prototypes of the URF model to a scale of 1:30.

Volker Küster also owns an outstanding model of a Swedish 'Najad' to the same scale. It is therefore possible to reproduce rescue manoeuvres with the model, which is a real incentive for ambitious submarine modellers to have a go at this project.

The construction of the prototypes certainly demanded some rethinking in contrast to the building of conventional model submarines. The submarine's hull consists of GRP and was made by first constructing a mould. The big challenge was to have the model steer as flexibly as the original. The URF has no adjustable steering planes. The main propulsion – a Maxon bell-armature geared motor drives the rigid screw via a water-proof magnetic coupling. The URF achieves its high degree of manoeuvrability by means of a lateral jet propulsion, built into both the stern and bow. These are assisted vertically by a jet lift incorporated in the middle of the submarine. The key feature of these drives is that they are two valve regulated rotary-pump drives. The valves are scratch built and relay controlled and enable the model to be turned on its vertical axis and somersault.

The main diving system consists of a proportionally controlled, piston ballast tank with a volume of 130 ml. The propulsion system is powered by ten NiMH Sub-C cells, developing 3,000 mAh and located in the stern. In the bow section there are four NiMH Mignon cells, developing 2,100 mAh to supply power to the receiver.

The prototypes successfully completed their first test dives and simulated docking manoeuvres; this confirmed the viability of the construction and propulsion concepts and it is now possible to begin to build more detailed models.

Technical data	
Scale	1:30
Length	470 mm
Width	105 mm
Height	140 mm
Displacement	approx. 3.3 kg

A view inside the stern and bow section of the URF. You can clearly see the pipes for the gyro-pump drives and the central bayonet ring lock.

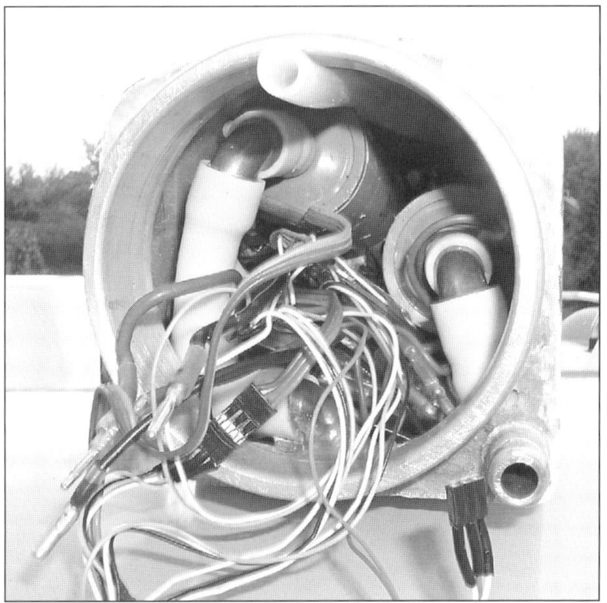

The 130 ml piston ballast tank.

The prototype's initial docking trials on Volker Küster's Swedish 'Najad', likewise built to a scale of 1:30.

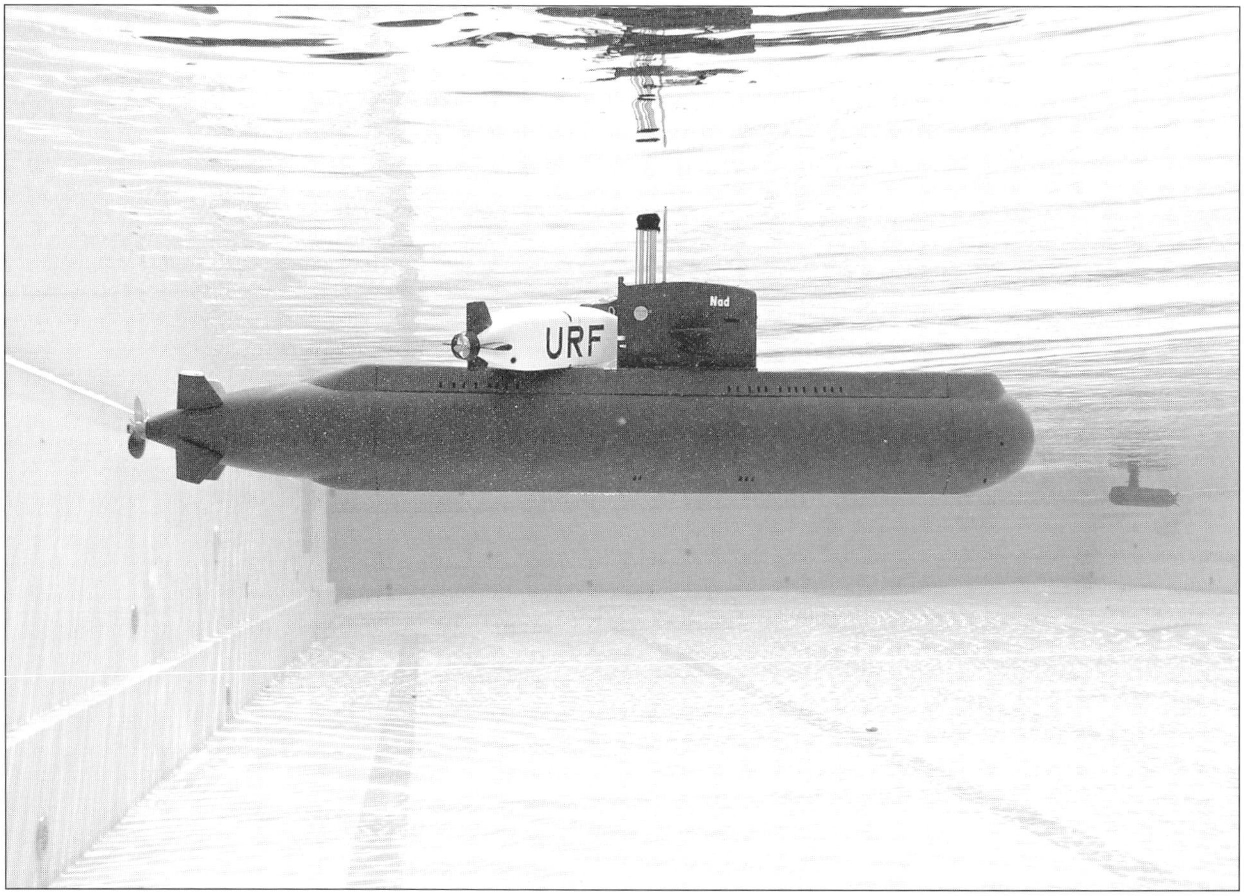

Chapter 11

Useful Addresses

You can find more information on the subject of model submarines on the following Internet sites. The list makes no pretence to be exhaustive.

International Modell U-Boot Verein SONAR. e.V
www.sonar-ev.de

Modell-U-Boot-Freunde Köln
www.ubootkoeln.de

The Subcommittee (USA)
www.subcommittee.com

Association of Modelsubmariners (GB)
www.modelsubmarines.org

Sub France (F)
www.multimania.com/subfrance

IG Modell U-Boote Austria (A)
www.igu-austria.org

The author's homepage:
www.diverteq.com

Sub Committee/SubComAust (Aus)
www.graysubs.tripod.com/home_page.htm

Norbert Brüggen Modell U-Boot Spezialitäten
www.modelluboot.de

Robbe Modellbau
www.robbe.com

Hasse Schiffsmodellbau
www.hassemodell.de

KMB Kehrer Modellbau Berlin
www.jet-drive.de

Klaus Krick Modelltechnik
www.krick-modell.de

Alexander Engel KG
www.engel-modellbau.de

Graupner Modellbau
www.graupner.de

Sources

Books, magazines etc:

Company literature ARGE U 212 HDW TNSW

Robert D. Ballard: Deep Sea – the Great Expeditions into the World of Eternal Darkness

Bruker company literature

Comex company literature

Hannes Ewerth: Die U-bootflotille der deutschen Marine

Harald Fock: Marine Kleinkampfmittel

Norbert Gierschner: Tauchboote

Norbert Gierschner: Tauchfahrzeuge

Typically HAUX, Haux Publishing

HDW AG: Silent Fleet, the German Designed Submarine Family

K. Herold: Der Kieler Brandtaucher

Paul Kemp: Manned Torpedoes and Midget Submarines

H.J Lawrence: The History of Submarines

Stefan Lipsky: Fazination U-boot – Museums-Unterseeboote aus aller Welt

Manned Submersible Engineering, Gerhard Haux Best Publishing Company

David Miller/John Jordan: Modern Submarines

Gosport museum guide

L. Nohse/E. Rössler: Konstruktionen für die Welt, Geschichte der Gabler-Unternehmen IKL and MG.

Antony Preston: The History of Submarines

Eberhard Rössler: Geschichte der deutschen U-bootbaus Band II

Eberhard Rössler/Fritz Köhl: Vom Original zum Modell U-Boottyp XXIII

Eberhard Rössler/H.J. Emsmann: Vom Original zum Modell U-Bootklasse 205

Ship Profiles: Nuclear Submarines of the USSR and Russia.

Jeffrey Tall: Submarines and Deep-Sea Vehicles

Notes

Notes

SAIL AWAY WITH OUR EXCITING RANGE OF BOOKS, VIDEOS AND DVDS

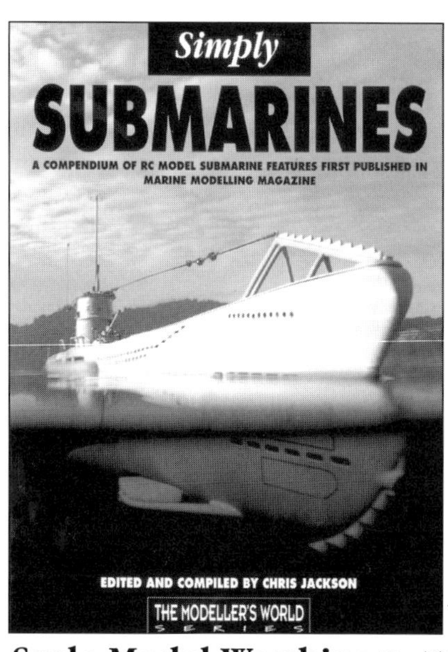

SIMPLY SUBMARINES
BY CHRIS JACKSON

A compilation of features first published in Marine Modelling International magazine, covering a wide range of different models, all explained in a simple and well illustrated style. An ideal starting point for beginners and with lots of building tips for the more experienced modeller.

Ref: SIMP £9.95/US $15.50 each + p&p/s&h

Scale Model Warships By Tim Morgan

This book covers selection and suitability of subject, plans and research, specialist suppliers, hulls and decks, working in plastic and brass, construction of superstructures, fittings, finishing and painting with emphasis on modern ships and up to date modelling methods.

Ref: SMW £12.95/US $22.00 each + p&p/s&h

SCALE MODEL BOATS
BY JOHN COX

A wealth of information which sets out the possibilities from the simplest construction to the most advanced. There's hints, tips and background information to help you get the maximum enjoyment from the building and operating of scale model boats.

Ref: SMB
£9.95/US $15.50 each + p&p/s&h